First and Quincy?

A. Well, she is supposed to be there at eight o'clock and

    which she has been, in many instances, but many times she

    has had to wait through the cold, the rain and the snow

    until the bus got there, not knowing definitely what time

    it gets there all the time.

Q. All right. Now, Mr. Brown, she boards that bus about

    eight o'clock. What time does she arrive at the school?

A. She's supposed to arrive at the school around 8:30.

Q. Eight thirty. And, as I understand it, what time does

    the classes begin at school?

A. Nine o'clock.

Q. What does your daughter do between the time the bus ar-

    rives at the school at 8:30 and 9:00 o'clock?

A. Well, there is sometimes she has had to wait outside the

    school until someone came to let them in, through the

    winter season and likewise, many times.

Q. What else does she do, if anything?

A. Well, there is nothing she can do except stand out and

    clap her hands to keep them warm or jump up and down.

    They have no provisions at all to shelter them.

Q. And what you want the Court to understand is that your

    daughter is conveyed to the school, she gets there by

    8:30 in the morning, and that she has nothing to do until

    school starts at 9:00 o'clock, is that right?

Kevin~ It
has been our
honor to work
with you these
last fourteen
years!!
Most Respectfully
& Sincerely~
Barb & Jenny
2007

GREAT PLAINS
ORIGINALS

GREAT PLAINS ORIGINALS

Historic documents from America's Heartland

Brian Burnes

★ KANSAS CITY STAR BOOKS
Kansas City, Missouri

To Debra, Charlie, Jessica and Sam: Thanks for letting me do all those things now that I wasn't able to do for the last several months. — BB

Published by Kansas City Star Books
1729 Grand Boulevard
Kansas City, Missouri 64108
Kansascity.com

First edition

ISBN-10: 1-933466-20-0
ISBN-13: 978-1-933466-20-0

Library of Congress Control Number: 2006936904

Editor: Monroe Dodd
Design: Kelly Ludwig and Leslie Beck, Ludwig Design, Inc.

Printed in the United States of America
by Walsworth Publishing Inc.
Marceline, Missouri

Contents

9-610

FROM THE NATIONAL ARCHIVES

Great Plains Originals: Historic Documents from America's Heartland depicts the struggles, challenges, triumphs, and personalities of the people inhabiting America's Great Plains. This perspective is unique and fresh; its authenticity rests in its source: the National Archives and Records Administration (NARA).

The National Archives houses and preserves the records of the federal government and our nation. In this role, it supports democracy, promotes civic literacy in America, and facilitates historical understanding of the national experience.

Our daily work is that of processing, preserving, and providing access to the federal documents that possess enduring historical or legal value. Such records include the Declaration of Independence, the Constitution, the Bill of Rights, military service records, immigration documents, federal court case files, millions of documents that protect the rights and entitlements of citizens, and many more records that tell the story of our nation and its people. In addition to assisting federal agencies and the public with research and reference services, the National Archives delivers educational programs to help Americans learn how to use archived records. By using archives, citizens can locate personal stories in our nation's documented history and, more importantly, find information that bears upon government accountability and the protection of citizens' individual rights.

Information found in documents, images, and reported accounts reflects the national character, our aspirations, and unique realities in local communities. The documents and primary sources held in trust at NARA locations nationwide tell powerful stories and offer compelling testimony of the impact of the federal government on the social, economic, cultural, and technological development of the United States.

Promulgated, codified, and interpreted by elected officials and civil servants in the nation's capital, federal government policies often are implemented and enforced through a network of federal field offices and district courts. Records created by these local offices and courts within regions document the many ways that policies were put into practice and how they affected everyday lives of Americans in those regions.

The documents selected for this publication are representative of the records of government offices located in the American heartland: the Great Plains. Taken from the holdings of the National Archives' Central Plains Region, serving federal offices and courts in Iowa, Kansas, Missouri, and Nebraska and including records from the Dakotas and Minnesota, these documents illustrate the many ways that government policy affected life upon the Great Plains.

For example, the Homestead Act of 1862 fostered the settlement and development of this vast region and is documented in the records of the General Land Office. The drama of the "American Experience" in the region is likewise revealed in the compensation claim files of Missouri slave owners who allowed their slaves to enlist in the United States Army. The registration forms of thousands of "female aliens"—native-born American women married to non-citizen German Americans—tell another unique story of wartime America. And the trial court cases of anti-war socialists Kate Richards O'Hare and Rose Pastor Stokes reveal the impact of the Espionage Act of 1917. The origins of an American icon, Mickey Mouse, can be traced to a time and a place in Kansas City among court records relating to Walt Disney.

I hope that the examples of records and their stories told in *Great Plains Originals* will inspire your interest in exploring further American themes as reflected in the vast holdings of National Archives facilities located throughout the nation or online at htpp://www.archives.gov. In addition to Kansas City, you can explore the resources at National Archives locations in Anchorage, Atlanta, Boston and Pittsfield (Massachusetts), Chicago, Denver, Fort Worth, Los Angeles/ Orange County, New York City, Philadelphia, Seattle, San Francisco, and St. Louis. I also invite you to visit NARA's eleven Presidential Libraries, which hold and display Presidential records and artifacts representing administrations from Hoover through Clinton, and our Washington, D.C. facilities—especially the National Archives Building where the Declaration of Independence, the Constitution of the United States, and the Bill of Rights are protected and on display along with thousands of other documents in our new Public Vaults Exhibit.

Great Plains Originals affords you the opportunity to visit the marvelous history in America's heartland through the records of the Central Plains Region. I know you will enjoy the journey.

ALLEN WEINSTEIN
Archivist of the United States

INTRODUCTION

The last scene of the movie "Raiders of the Lost Ark" resembles the first thing staff archivists see every day when they come to work. Before them sprawls a vast storeroom, housing thousands of boxes, stretching seemingly to infinity.

Here, in the heart of the country, at the Central Plains Region branch of the National Archives, are 50,000 cubic feet of documents. They were generated by about 90 federal agencies from across the Great Plains, and they date back decades. Some were produced long before 1934, when the National Archives was established.

Most are one of a kind. The people and events they describe range from pivotal to obscure to plain mysterious. Each letter, picture, court file or artifact must be retrievable by an archives staff member.

That's the difference between "Raiders" and real life.

The archives represent a unique place on the cultural map of the Great Plains. Here, in Kansas City, Missouri, Americans can look back into their collective and individual past.

A visitor asks for information, the files are produced, the visitor signs for them and begins perusing. At first glance, the records seem routine.

- A Selective Service card filled out in the early 1940s by a 58-year-old man.
- A form on which a property owner claims title to an asset lost in the Civil War.
- A note from a 19th-century Army officer notifying a quartermaster official that a carload of trains and mules is headed his way.

But look closer.

- The draft card belonged to Harry S. Truman, then a U.S. senator and just a few years from becoming president of the United States.
- That property owner wanted the government to reimburse him for a human being – a slave who enlisted in the U.S. Army.
- The Army officer's note bears the signature of George Armstrong Custer.

At the archives, one visit isn't enough. Sometimes, documents are fragmentary. It's as if they dare a visitor to find the rest of the story.

Surprises happen. Archivists know where groups of records are, but they don't know the precise contents of every box. Any day may be Christmas morning.

Most legal records, for example, are stored in Record Group 21, Records of the District Courts of the United States. The contents run from 1822 through the 1990s and fill more than 25,000 cubic feet. Some boxes may not have been examined in recent memory. If you're willing to blaze your own trail, a vast forest awaits.

The storage of federal papers in Kansas City goes back to about 1950. That's when the Federal Records Depository opened in the Fairfax Industrial District in Wyandotte County, Kansas. When the Kansas River flooded in July 1951 about 12 feet of water poured into the depository. Records were moved to rented space, and then later to Bannister Road in south Kansas City, Missouri, to a new warehouse shared with the General Services Administration.

Eventually, that became the home of the Kansas City Federal Records Center, a branch of the newly established National Archives and Records Service, successor to a U.S. Army records center in Kansas City. After World War II, Kansas City had housed some captured documents, among them the diary of Eva Braun, companion of Adolf Hitler. (The diary is no longer kept in Kansas City. In 1969 the Kansas City records center sent it and other classified Army documents to Washington in a sealed train with an armed Military Police escort.)

The regional archives was established as a branch of the Kansas City Federal Records Center in 1969. In its earliest days the archives held perhaps 200 cubic feet of records. Through the years the records kept arriving, and the center established an advisory board of about 100 historians and scholars eager to see the regional archives expand. Many board members were university professors, but the archives soon attracted a new constituency: genealogists.

In the early 1970s federal officials transferred to the Kansas City branch a collection of microfilmed U.S. Censuses. That brought the

Storage files at the National Archives' Central Plains Region in the 1970s

genealogists, whose numbers swelled in the 1970s with the appearance of *Roots*, the book by Alex Haley, and the television mini-series based on it. In 1983 the branch established the first regional volunteer program. Volunteers answer questions about genealogy resources and the branch's holdings.

Today, the Central Plains Region holds the retired records of federal agencies that operated in Iowa, Kansas, Minnesota, Missouri, Nebraska, North Dakota and South Dakota.

Inside all those boxes lie star attractions — Wild West showman "Buffalo Bill" Cody, the transcript of *Brown v. Board of Education of Topeka*, native American leader Sitting Bull, and Perry Smith, who was hanged for the Clutter murders and was the subject of *In Cold Blood* — along with fascinating sidetrips into the whimsy, the mystery and the history of the Great Plains.

— Brian Burnes

Hd. Qrs Fort Lincoln D.T.
May 9th 1875—

Captain T. J. Eckerson
    A. Q. M. U.S. Army
        Sir—
            In reply to your letter the
Bvt Major General Commanding desires me
to inform you that he does not consider it
advisable to order the Guard at Camp
Hancock to supply you with water, as
their duties are such that their presence
is required at all times at the Camp—
            Very respectfully
                your obdt. servt.
                    James Calhoun
                    1 St Lt
                    Adjutant

Emma Sheppard, Ind.
Baker,
Chey. River Sch. S.D.
Apr. 30, 1915

THE WEST

**The Old West comes alive in the
Central Plains Region archives.**

From the mundane to the murderous, details
surrounding the lives and fates of William F. "Buffalo
Bill" Cody, Sitting Bull, George Armstrong Custer
and Wild Bill Hickok are all here. Records of the
Bureau of Indian Affairs going back to the 19th century
attract scholars from around the world for their
accounts of the transformation of Native American
life as white settlement moved across the frontier.

Just Routine

Even if you had a rendezvous with destiny, you still had to submit the proper paperwork to get a barrel of oysters, arrange for steamboat transportation, or record shipments of mules and horses.

So it was with George Armstrong Custer and members of his Seventh Calvary who fought in the June 1876 Battle of the Little Bighorn.

For the 130th anniversary of the battle in 2006, staff members of the Central Plains Region assembled documents from the quartermaster depot at Bismarck, Dakota Territory, which was responsible for the procurement and distribution of Army supplies. The workaday papers were generated by Custer as well as officers James C. Calhoun, Custer's brother-in-law, and Myles Keogh — all of whom died at Little Bighorn. Still others were signed by survivors, among them officers Marcus A. Reno and Frederick Benteen.

All the documents were from the Office of the Quartermaster General, part of material recently received from Washington in an effort to make more original documents available to researchers in regional archives.

George Armstrong Custer discusses the movement of
mules, below, and Myles Keogh requests a ferry for a
troop of cavalry, its horses and wagons, left.
Record Group 92

Battalion 7th Cavalry
mark D. T.
May 4th 187[?]

Qr. Mr. U. S.
Bismark

request that y[ou]
tation from [?]
[?]ala D. T. for
[?]venteen (117) En[?]
ty three public
(2) wagons.

[?]fully
[?]
W. Keogh
[?] 7th Cavalr[y]
Commanding

C. H. HASKINS, Gen'l Sup't,
MILWAUKEE, WIS.

Z. G. SIMMONS, Pres't,
H. B. HINSDALE, Sec'y,

KENOSHA, WIS.

Dated ___ Fargo '10 ___ 187 4
Received at ___ Bismer 116
To ___ Col Bradley
        A. Q. M. Bismarck D T

One car load of mules
and one of horses in
to days train. I have telegraphed
Dandy to have them ferried
across this evening if you
get them down to River

G. A. Custer
Bvt Major Genl

Collect 41

WILD BILL'S KILLER

Deadwood, Dakota Territory, won lasting fame on August 2, 1876, when Jack McCall murdered James Butler Hickok — better known as "Wild Bill" Hickok.

At his first trial, McCall was acquitted. However, federal authorities stepped in and took McCall to the territorial capital at Yankton, where a second trial was held. The indictment against McCall was full of proper language, maintaining how McCall — by using "a certain revolver or pistol then and there charged with gunpowder" had killed Hickok, who was famous for his days as a U.S. Army scout, a federal marshal in Kansas, and performer with Buffalo Bill's Wild West Show.

The second time, McCall was convicted and sentenced to death. He was hanged on March 1, 1877.

Excerpts from the minutely detailed indictment of Jack McCall, next two pages, followed by McCall's defense. He was, he said, "in such a state of intoxication that whilst crossing the street in Deadwood he fell three different times."

Record Group 21

"United States of America, }
Territory of Dakota.

In District Court in and for the Second
Judicial District.   October Term, 1876.

The United States,   }
        vs.   } Indictment for Murder.
John McCall, alias   }
Jack McCall.   }

The Grand Jurors of the United States of
America, within and for the Second Judicial
District of Dakota Territory, upon their oaths
present that on the second day of August, in
the year of our Lord One thousand, eight
hundred and seventy-six, in the Sioux Indian
Reservation set apart under the treaty proclaim-
ed February 24th, 1869, at a place in said
Reservation called Deadwood, in said District
and Territory, said Reservation then and there
being in the Indian Country and a place
within the sole and exclusive jurisdiction of
the United States, and within the jurisdiction
of this Court, one John McCall, alias Jack
McCall, late of said District and Territory,
yeoman, with force and arms, in and upon
one, William Hickock, whose Christian name to said

pistol he the said John McCall, alias Jack Mc
Call in his right hand then and there had
and held, at and against the said, ~William~ Hickock,
~whose Christian name is to said jurors unknown,~
alias Wild Bill, then and there feloniously, wil
fully and of his malice aforethought did shoot
off and discharge; and that the said John
McCall alias Jack McCall, with the leaden
bullet aforsaid, by means of shooting off
and discharging the said revolver pistol, so
loaded, to, at and against the said, ~William~ Hickock
~whose Christian name is to said jurors unknown,~ alias Wild Bill, as aforesaid, did
then and there feloniously, wilfully and of
his malice aforethought strike, penetrate and
wound the said, ~William~ Hickock, ~whose Christian name~
~is to said jurors unknown,~ alias Wild Bill
in and through the head of him the said, ~William~ Hickock, ~whose Christian name is to said jurors~
~unknown,~ alias Wild Bill, giving him the
said, ~William~ Hickock, ~whose Christian name is to said~
~jurors unknown,~ alias Wild Bill, then and
there, with the leaden bullet aforesaid, by
means of shooting off and discharging the
said revolver pistol so loaded, to, at and
against the said, ~William~ Hickock, ~whose Christian~
~name is to said jurors unknown,~ alias Wild
Bill, and by such striking ~penetrating~ and wounding
the said, ~William~ Hickock, ~whose Christian name is~

CHICAGO

The United States   Oct. Term. 1876.

      vs.   In United States Dist. Court

John McCall, alias   2nd Judicial Dist. Dakota Ter.

Jack McCall.   SS. Indictment for Murder.

      The Defendant above being first duly sworn doth depose and say, that he cannot go safely to trial at this term of court on account of the unavoidable absence of important and material witnesses, That after the alleged homicide he was arrested at Laramie City in the Territory of Wyoming, immediately placed in custody and forthwith brought to Yankton and has held since in close custody, without any opportunity to get witnesses or prepare a defense; that he is poor and unable to employ officers or furnish means for the procurement of witnesses himself, That John Weldon and Daniel Boyd are material witnesses in his defense to prove that J. B. Hickok, alias Wild Bill, was a desperado of the worst character, addicted to violence and whose frequent quent boast it was that he was the slayer of thirty men, and that at the time of the alleged homicide he was in pursuit of the deponent as his thirty-first victim.

will swear that deponent at the time
of the alleged homicide was in such a state
of intoxication that whilst crossing the
street in Deadwood he fell three different
times, and was in such a state of insen-
sibility from the effects of liquor as to ren-
der him unconscious of moral responsibility
and legal accountability. That the above
named witnesses and —— Barker and many
others would swear that at the time of this
alleged homicide there existed in the Deadwood,
and in the whole region of the Black Hills about
there, a state of great public excitement, violence
and personal danger, that shooting affrays
were frequent and a ssomthreaten threat
to take life was ominous of a certain attempt to do so, and that only the day previous
to this alleged homicide the said Wild Bill
was engaged in an affair with pistols with
a certain man in Deadwood named Barker
whose Christian name is to this deponent unknown.

Deponent therefor, for the foregoing reasons,
and on account of this being the first time after
the arrest asks that in justice to himself the
case may be continued to the next
term of this Court, that he may be en—

Yankton, D.T. Dec 6th 1876

We, the jurors in the case of the United States vs. John McCall alias Jack McCall find a verdict of Guilty of Murder as charged in the indictment.

John Treadway, Forman — John Treadway, Forman

Charles H. Edwards, Secretary — Charles H. Edwards, Secretary

George Pike — George Pike.

Martin L. Hinckel — Martin L. Winchel.

Henry T. Mowry — Henry T. Mowry.

Hiram A. Dunham — Hiram A. Dunham.

Lewis Clark — Lewis Colenk

West Negus — West Negus

William Box — William Box

Isaac N. Esmay — Isaac N. Esmay.

Nelson Armstrong — Nelson Armstrong.

J. A. Withee — J A Withee

SEIZED!

On Dec. 15, 1890, Sitting Bull — the Hunkpapa Lakota chief whose warriors in 1876 destroyed the cavalry of George Armstrong Custer — died in an attempt by Indian police to arrest him. His death at the Standing Rock Indian Agency, or reservation, in the Dakotas helped symbolize the end of the Plains Indian era of the 19th Century.

Sitting Bull was living at the Standing Rock reservation, which today straddles the boundary of South and North Dakota. In 1889 American authorities had grown concerned about a messianic movement among some American Indians that promised an Indian messiah would arise and return them to their earlier dominance of the plains. A ritual called the Ghost Dance symbolized the movement.

Amid fears that Sitting Bull would promote the movement, Standing Rock Agent James McLaughlin in December 1890 ordered his arrest.

McLaughlin wrote that the arrest could be made "by the Indian Police without much risk." McLaughlin noted a variety of security measures that he had taken and added: "You must not let him escape under any circumstances." Sitting Bull was shot to death in a gunfight between his followers and the Indian police.

Through more than a century, the letter that triggered Sitting Bull's death took a circuitous and somewhat mysterious path to the archives at the Central Plains Region.

Many records of the federal government Indian reservation system were transferred formally to the National Archives in the 1950s and 1960s. Occasionally, archives staff members noticed records that couldn't be accounted for. Sometimes such records turned up in forgotten storerooms — and sometimes outside federal authority.

That's what happened with McLaughlin's letter. Papers created by the agent around 1890 seemed to have vanished from federal custody around the time of World War I. Staff members at the Central Plains Region believe they were given to an acquaintance of a McLaughlin descendant.

Recently a staff member noticed that the McLaughlin records were being offered for sale by an online auction service. National Archives personnel contacted the auction service, whose operators willingly surrendered the volumes to the archives' Seattle branch.

In April 2006 a Seattle archives staff member brought the volumes to a conference in Los Angeles and delivered them to a Central Plains staff member. They are now held in the branch's collection of documents from the Standing Rock agency.

A series of letters, one translated, surrounding the arrest of Sitting Bull.
Record Group 75

12<u>30</u> A.M.

Grand River, Dec 14th 1890

Maj James McLaughlin
Standing Rock Agcy
N.D.

Dear Sir:—

"Bull Head," wishes to report what
occured at S. B's Camp at a Council held yesterday.
It seems that Sit Bull has received a letter from
the Pine Ridge outfit, asking him to come over
there, as God was to appear to them, S B's people
want him to go, but he has sent a letter to you
asking your permission, and if you do not
give it, he is going to go anyway, he has been
fitting up his horses, to stand a long ride
and will go a horseback in case he is pursued
Bull Head would like to arrest him at once
before he has the chance of giving them the
slip, as he thinks that if he gets the start, it
will be impossible to catch him, if you should
want to arrest him, he says to send word to
him by courier immediatly, also to let him
know what your plans are, if Soldiers
are to come, he says to send them by S. B's
Road. — He also mentions something
about "Shave Head" coming down here
but as I am not good enough interpreter
to understand Everything he has said

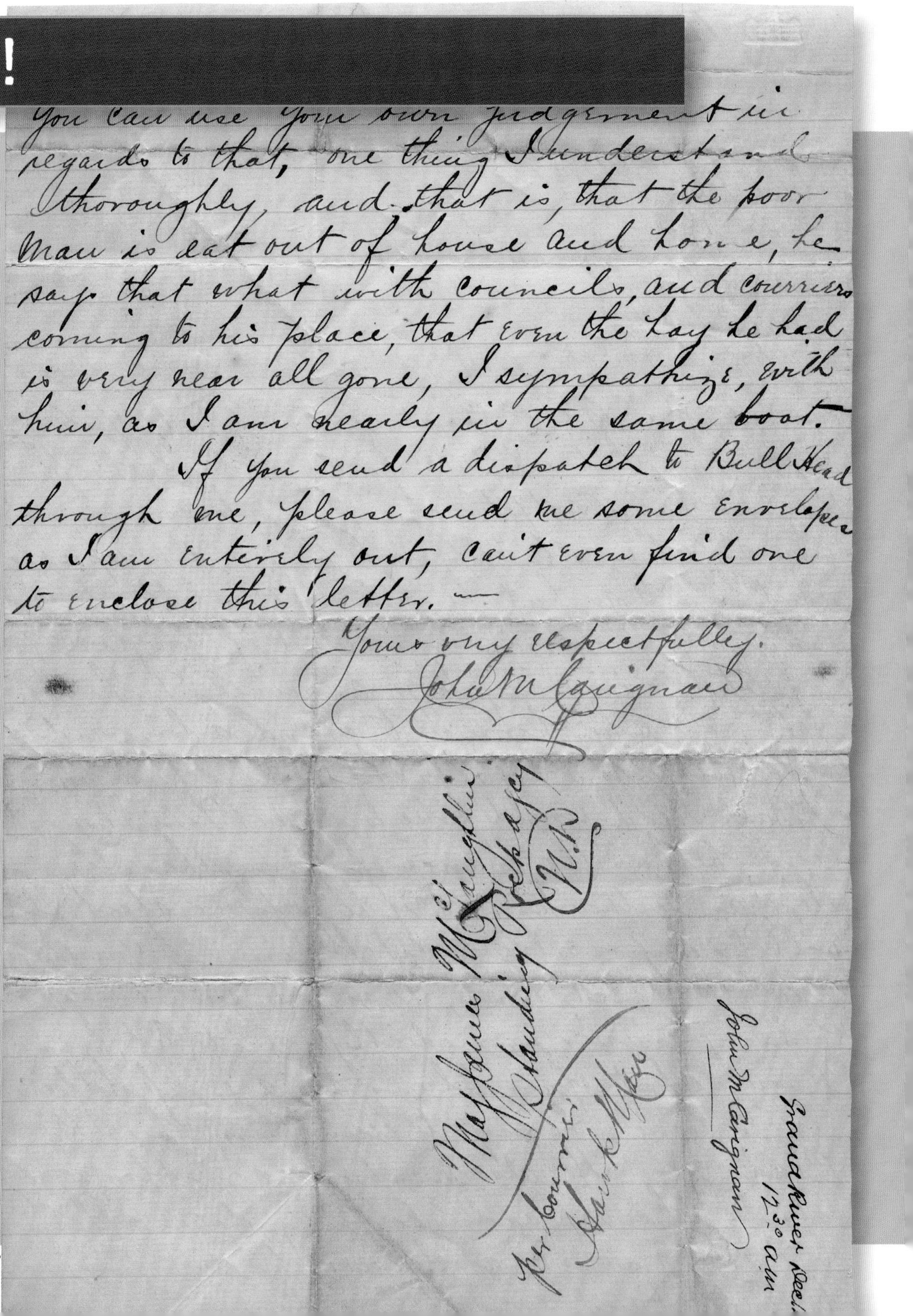

You can use your own judgement in regards to that, one thing I understand thoroughly, and that is, that the poor man is eat out of house and home, he says that what with councils, and courriers coming to his place, that even the hay he had is very near all gone, I sympathize, with him, as I am nearly in the same boat.

If you send a dispatch to Bull Head through me, please send me some Envelopes as I am entirely out, can't even find one to enclose this letter. —

Yours very respectfully.

John M Carignan

McLaughlin et
McLaughlin Agency
U.S.

MajJames McLaughlin

Per Courrier

Peter B Mac

John M Carignan

Grand River Red.
12.30 am

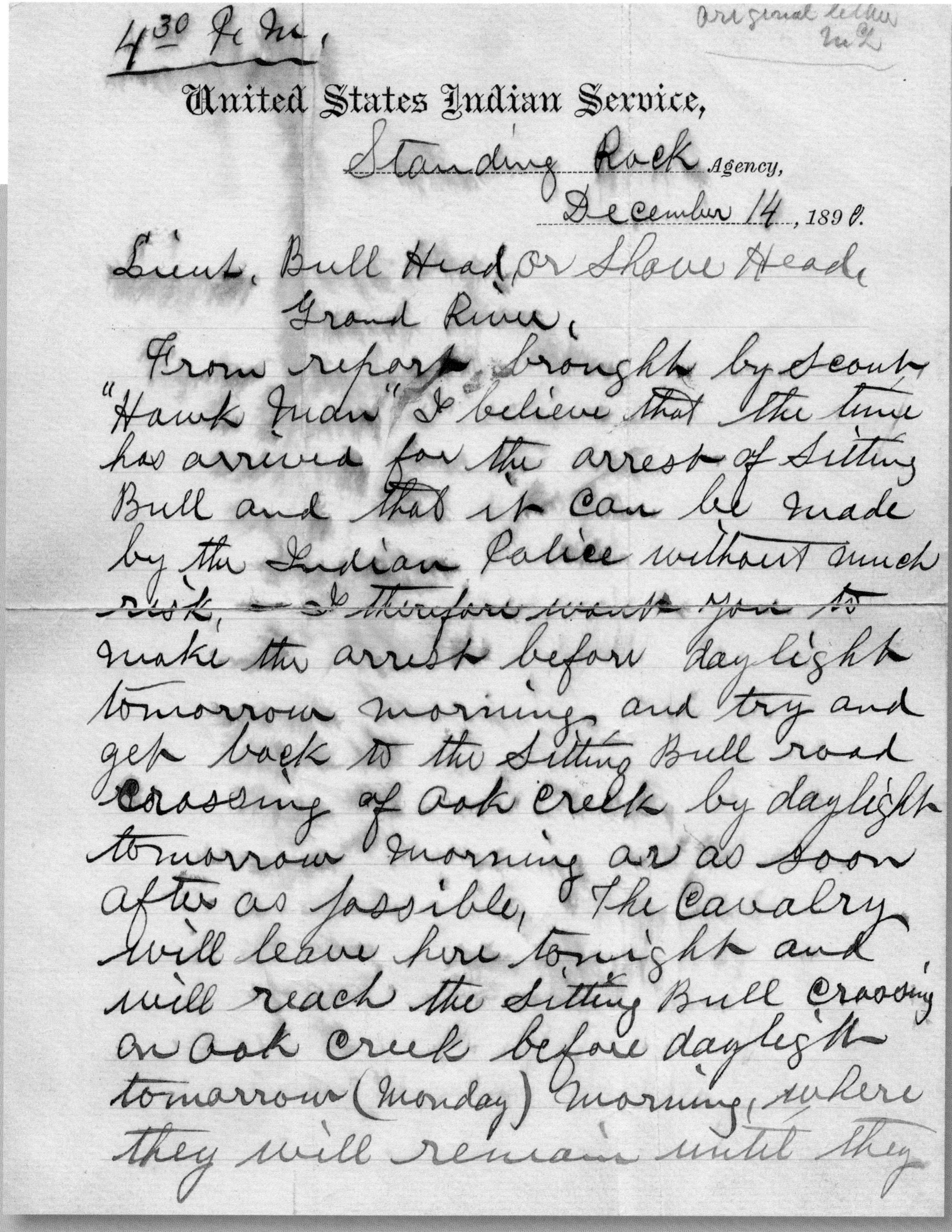

4³⁰ P.m.,

United States Indian Service,

Standing Rock Agency,

December 14, 1890.

Lieut. Bull Head or Shave Head
Grand River,

From reports brought by scout
"Hawk Man" I believe that the time
has arrived for the arrest of Sitting
Bull and that it can be made
by the Indian Police without much
risk, — I therefore want you to
make the arrest before daylight
tomorrow morning, and try and
get back to the Sitting Bull road
crossing of Oak creek by daylight
tomorrow morning or as soon
after as possible, The Cavalry
will leave here tonight and
will reach the Sitting Bull crossing
on Oak creek before daylight
tomorrow (Monday) morning, where
they will remain until they

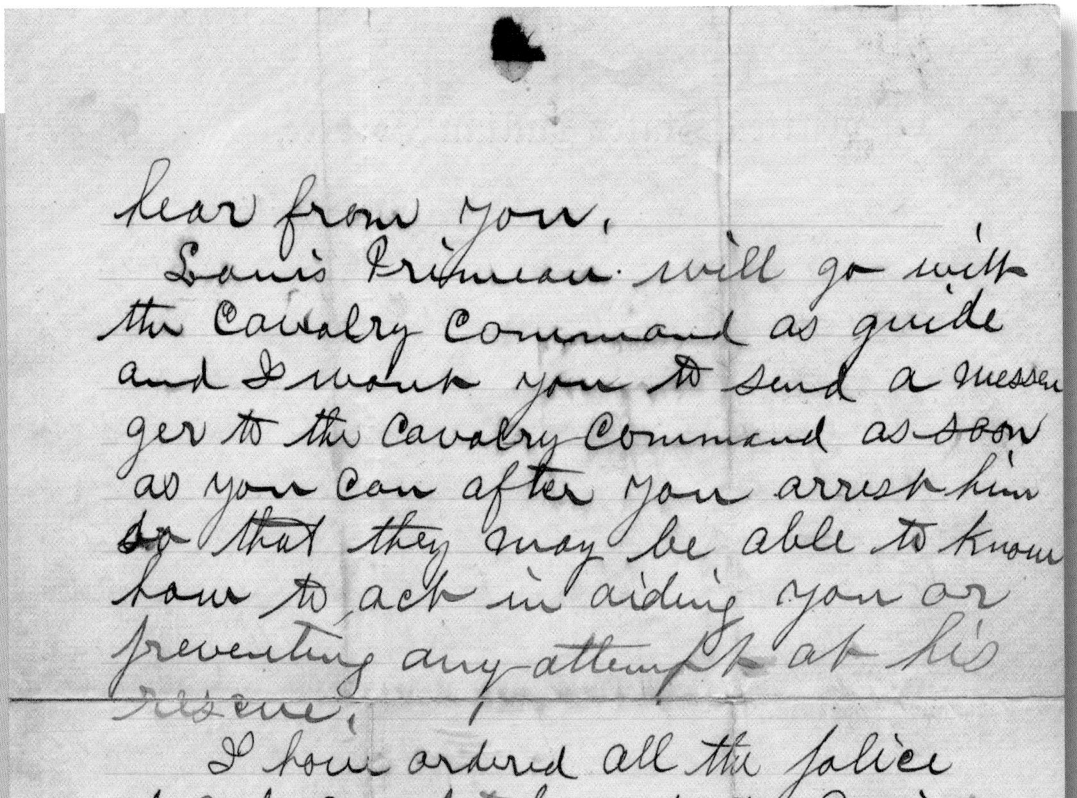

hear from you.

Louis Primeau will go with
the Cavalry Command as guide
and I want you to send a messen
ger to the Cavalry Command as soon
as you can after you arrest him
so that they may be able to know
how to act in aiding you or
preventing any attempt at his
rescue.

I have ordered all the police
at Oak Creek to proceed to Carignans
School to await your orders, this
gives you a force of 42 Policemen
for to use in the arrest.

Very respectfully
James McLaughlin
Wiss Inde Agt

P.S.
You must not let him escape
under any circumstances.

original letter-
J.B.W.

Standing Rock Agency
Dec. 14/90

Matokipaki qa kasla.

Citanwicaxa wowapi
wan makihi kin iwacu yunkan
wanna Tatankaiyotanka oyuxapi
kte cin eyehan unkipi iblukcan
ye lo, Unkiknakapi ehantans
chan iyaye ~~chas~~ ~~iyaye~~ unyanpi
kta ikowape lo; Ca lehan le han-
hepi kin wanna el lapi qa
anpaosni ecel oluxapi kte lo
Tokesa Luwitanka asucita kin
om yinkte lo, qa canku wan
yake cin okna yapi qa
ituhu oju oiyuwege kin hel
enajin kte, Tatanka iyotanke qa
ibgleska tacanku oiyuwege kin
hel wake lo, el tipi kao uni
sipi kin hel anipe najin pi
kte lo ca toke tu ehantans hel
orankoya wanji hosi yahipi
kte lo,

Ateyaki kin muje
ca he pe lo

WOUNDED KNEE

Still worried about the Ghost Dance movement among American Indians, U.S. authorities on December 29, 1890, set out to arrest more leaders. The result was the Wounded Knee Massacre, called the last U.S. military action against Native Americans.

When attempts were made to arrest one American Indian leader and his followers at their camp, gunfire broke out. By the time the shooting stopped, 150 to 300 American Indians were dead.

Bureau of Indian Affairs records at the Central Plains Region contain a 1928 transcript of the massacre by participant John Ghost Bear.

Transcript of John Ghost Bear's account of the Wounded Knee Massacre.

Record Group 75

PINE RIDGE AGENCY,
PINE RIDGE, SOUTH DAKOTA,
November 1, 1928.

The Indians who took part in the Wounded Knee bat
were what was known as the Big Foot Band, who lived on
Cheyenne River, about twenty-five miles, above the mout
Cherry Creek and six miles below the mouth of the Bell
Fourche River.

Big Foot had something like 350 Indians with him,
cluding men, women and children; and they left home ab
the middle of December, 1890, presumably to join the h
tile Indians who were on the Pine Ridge Reservation.

General Miles was in command of all the soldiers
Indian scouts on the Pine Ridge Reservation; and he he
that the Big Foot Band of Indians were coming, and sen
a troop of cavalry, under Major Adams, and several India
scouts, to head them off before they came to White Riv
but, before the soldiers got to what is now called the
Foot Pass, the Indians had gone down, so Major Adams a
his soldiers and scouts came down the pass after the In
dians, but there were too many of the Indians; so he j
followed them towards Pine Ridge, and did not attempt
head them off or stop them.

General Miles heard that Major Adams had not succe
ed in heading the Indians off, so he sent five troops
the 7th cavalry to meet them and bring them to Pine Rid
so they could not join the hostile Indians. The soldier
met the Indians at Porcupine Butte, and brought them d
to Wounded Knee Creek, where they camped for the night.

It was decided to disarm the Indians at Wounded Kn
before they brought them to Pine Ridge; so the Indians
lined up, and the soldiers started to take the guns awa
from them. Most of the soldiers were placed on small hi
around where the Indians were lined up, and the artille
was on the small hill where the Indians that were kille
in the fight are now buried. There were five field guns
and a Gatling gun placed on this hill. The soldiers we
ordered to fire on the Indians, if they did not give up
their arms peaceably.

After most of the Indians were disarmed, Lieutenant Wallace stepped over to an Indian named Slippery Skin, who was not in the line, and Slippery Skin shot and killed Lieutenant Wallace. That started the fight, and the Indians started to run, most of them up the large draw, just South of where the Indians were being disarmed.

The fight lasted about two hours. There were about 170 Indians killed, including women and children; and there were more women and children killed than there were men. There were about 35 soldiers killed, presumably most of them having been shot by each other, as nearly, if not quite, all of the Indians had been disarmed. A few of the Indian men picked up the guns of the soldiers that had been killed, and used them to fight the soldiers; but most of them had nothing to fight with. Colonel Forsythe was in immediate command of the soldiers who were in the fight. The fight took place December 29, 1890.

As told by John Ghost Bear, who was an Indian police on duty, and actually took part in the battle.

Interpreted by Ben Janis, who was an Indian scout during the Indian War of 1890-91.

On the Reservation

A huge volume of cattle brands compiled by the Pine Ridge Agency chief of police in 1910 listed a bewildering variety of cattle brands then in use on agency land.

Sometimes, livestock owners tried to graze unauthorized animals on land of American Indian agencies or reservations. Knowing which animals had been authorized required a repository of brands.

The big book listed each brand with its owner.
Record Group 75

Far right: Residents of the Cheyenne River Agency, from early in the 20th century. Top: John Black Hawk
Record Group 75

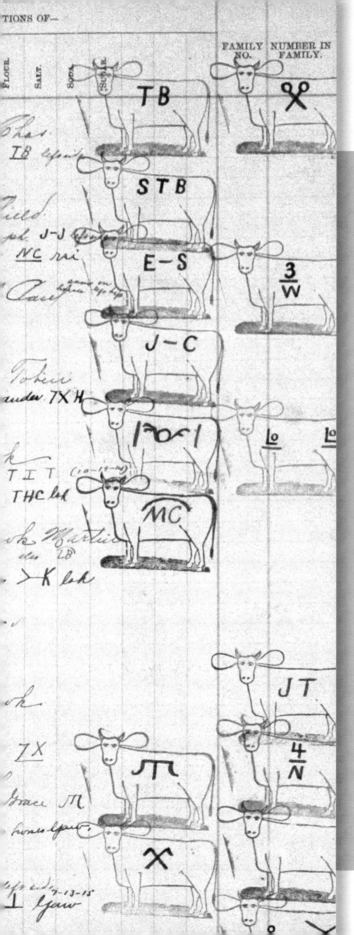

FLOUR. SALT. SOAP.

FAMILY NO.

NUMBER IN FAMILY.

Emma Sheppard, Ind.
Baker,
Chey. River Sch. S.D.
Apr. 30, 1915

Allen Fielder. Ind.
Line Rider,
Cheyenne River Agency
S.D.
Apr. 19, 1915

A SCHOOL FOR NATIVE AMERICANS

Haskell Indian Nations University in Lawrence, Kansas, traces its origins to 1884, when it offered agricultural education instruction for grades one through five.

The institution's early name was the United States Indian Industrial Training School. In about 10 years a "normal" school was added because teachers were needed in the communities from which the students came. By 1927 high school classes at Haskell were accredited by the state of Kansas.

Haskell files at the Central Plains Region show students from various tribes receiving mechanical and medical instruction, dressed for baseball and participating in theatrical productions.

In 1970 Haskell began offering a junior college curriculum. In 1992, the school's board selected a new name, Haskell Indian Nations University, to reflect its envisioned role as a national center for American Indian education and research.

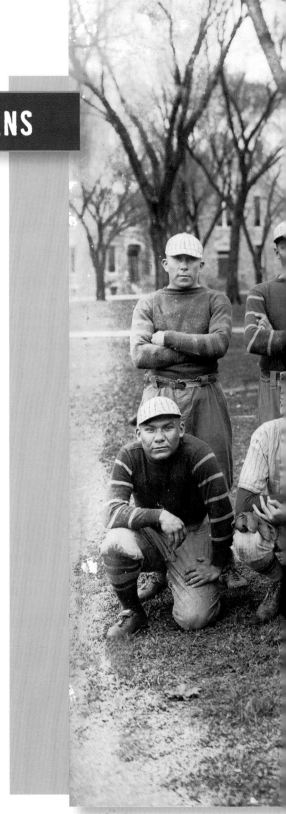

All set to play baseball at Haskell.
Record Group 75

Haskell students in the dispensary, left, and in military dress, above.
Record Group 75

At another Indian school, Armstrong Academy in southeast Oklahoma, students showed off homemade playground equipment in 1912.
Record Group 75

BUFFALO BILL'S EXTRAVAGANZAS

William F. "Buffalo Bill" Cody is said to have invented the American memory of the western frontier with his Wild West shows.

His production was conceived in the early 1880s and continued about 30 years. In 1887 he performed for Queen Victoria of England at her jubilee celebration. By 1913 his show was still running, by then affiliated with Sells-Floto circus company.

Cody performed in the Wild West productions and was an authentic attraction, being a former Pony Express rider, U.S. Army scout and buffalo hunter for employees of the Kansas Pacific Railroad.

His shows were spectacles. They required hundreds of players, and to achieve the authenticity that Cody desired he also needed Native American performers. For those, he contracted with the federal government.

Many of the Indians came from the Pine Ridge Indian agency. Cody's letters are full of details about who got paid, who was coming back to the agency soon and who might be expected to send money home to relatives.

One letter, from 1892, alerts an Army captain at Pine Ridge to the impending arrival of several Native Americans who had performed with Cody that season. Another letter, from 1913, includes Cody's plans for all Native Americans at the Pine Ridge agency who were still owed money for their performances to swear out claims.

"I would not bother you in this matter excepting that I know you, as well as I, want these Indians to receive all their money," Cody wrote an Army colonel at the agency.

Cody died in 1917.

Through the years, W. F. Cody's letters to Indian agents came on a panoply of letterheads.
Record Group 75

BUFFALO BILL'S
WILD WEST
COMBINED WITH
PAWNEE BILL'S GREAT
FAR EAST.

Glen Falls.
June 18th

Dear Col Brennan.

Colorado Sp

nen.
cy, S. D.

Major Brennen:-

g who has been

them.

I have informed the Indians who have been sending money to write & explain to you who the money was intended for. As they are going home so soon I hardly think they will send

BUFFALO BIL[L]
WILD W[EST]

COL. W. F. CODY - -
NATE SALSBURY - Vice
JNO. M. BURKE - -

August

Capt Geo Le Roy Brown,
United States Indian Ser
Pine Ridge Agenc[y]

dear Captain,

Your favor of Aug
to hand, which found
well here. We are all

Very sincerely

I am yours truly
W. F. Cody

Season 1914 :: ANNOUNCEMENT :: 1914 Season

BUFFALO BILL & SELLS-FLOTO CIRCUS
TWO GIGANTIC SHOWS
For TWENTY FIVE Cents Admission

The Season 1914 opens in March. The Sells-Floto Circus will continue to give its regular performances—added to it will be Buffalo Bill (Col. W. F. Cody), who will personally direct and play in his "Wild West;" also new and spectacular scenic production arranged by Frederic Thompson, builder, producer, manager of New York Luna Park, New York Hippodrome, Exposition Midway Exhibits and famous theatricals. 450 people and 300 horses will take part. The mechanical and scenic effects will be so unusual that the circus world will be astounded.

The seating capacity will be 14,000, making it larger than the largest.

Performers and others desiring engagements for 1914, also those who have novelties to offer, are invited to write to

THE SELLS-FLOTO SHOWS CO.
DENVER, COLORADO

GENERAL OFFICES, THE SELLS-FLOTO SHOWS CO.
237 SYMES BUILDING, DENVER, COLO.

WINTER QUARTERS, 26TH AVE. AND HAZEL COURT
NORTH DENVER

August 23, 1913.

Colonel John R. Brennan
Agent Pine Ridge Agency,
Pine Ridge, S. D.

My dear Colonel:

You, in all probability, know that the Indians through unfortunate circumstances have not received their money and as they all have preferred claims against the estate, I wish you would kindly have all the Indians come to your agency and have them swear to the claims.

I have arranged with Charles Redmond of this

REGISTRATION CARD—(Men born on or after April 28, 1877 and on or before Feb

SERIAL NUMBER	1. NAME (Print)		
U 4622	Harry	S	Truman
	(First)	(Middle)	(Last)

2. PLACE OF RESIDENCE (Print)

219 No Deleware, Independence Jacks

(Number and street)   (Town, township, village, or city)   (Co

[THE PLACE OF RESIDENCE GIVEN ON THE LINE ABOVE WILL DET
JURISDICTION; LINE 2 OF REGISTRATION CERTIFICATE WILL

3. MAILING ADDRESS

240 Senate Office Building, Washingto

[Mailing address if other than place indicated on line 2.   If same insert w

4. TELEPHONE	5. AGE IN YEARS	6.
Na. 3120	58	
	May 8, DATE OF BIRTH 1884	
(Exchange) (Number)	(Mo.) (Day) (Yr.)	

7. NAME AND ADDRESS OF PERSON WHO WILL ALWAYS KNOW YOUR ADDRESS

Bess W. Truman   219 No. Deleware

8. EMPLOYER'S NAME AND ADDRESS

United States Senate

9. PLACE OF EMPLOYMENT OR BUSINESS

Washington, D. C

(Number and street or R.F.D. number)   (Town)

I AFFIRM THAT I HAVE VERIFIED ABOVE ANSWERS AND THAT THEY ARE TRUE.

Harry T

D. S. S. Form 1   16—21630—2   (Regis

6, 1897)

MO.
(State)

E LOCAL BOARD
ENTICAL]

O. C

F BIRTH
r, MO
(Town or county)

(State or country)

ndependence, Mo

ckson, Mo.

(State)

nature)

2.

WAR AND ITS OFFSPRING

How the United States tested the loyalty of septuagenarians and Civil War vets, promoted home economics on the home front and hired "women of war" to make bombs on the prairie.

ENEMY ALIENS ALL

After the United States entered World War I in April 1917, non-naturalized natives of Germany were considered "alien enemy." By presidential proclamation, they had to register with local authorities. Even women of American birth had to register if they had married a non-naturalized German.

As part of the process, each "alien enemy" had to provide a photograph and fingerprints. Thousands of these registrations survive in the files of the Central Plains Region, and many of the registrants appear to represent only a slim threat to national security.

Consider Alberta Walburga, a 44-year-old native of Germany who lived in Wichita. She filled out and signed her affidavit in June 1918, listing her height at 4 feet 10 inches and weight at 110 pounds. She had arrived in the United States back in 1901, and since 1903 had worked at St. Francis Hospital in Wichita.

She conceded that she had three brothers who had taken up arms against the United States, presumably by being members of the German armed forces. Yet she had never taken an oath of allegiance to any other country and had never been arrested. In her picture she wore a traditional black and white habit, standard uniform for members of Catholic women's orders.

Alberta was a nun.

Similarly classed as alien enemy were Anna Eberth, Bertha Fromm, Magareth Fuchs, Mary Ebert, Josepha Goetz, Anna Gehring, Barbra Foertch and other nuns who worked at St. Francis. Each signed her affidavit, giving proof, as the form said, of their "peaceful disposition" and their intention to abide by the laws of the United States. Most faced the camera in the same manner, with eyes downcast. Was it resignation at being classed as an enemy of the United States?

The taking of fingerprints, the form added, was not to be "deemed an imputation that the registrant is not a law-abiding person." Nevertheless, fingerprints were taken.

The Central Plains Region has 5,929 Kansas affidavits, evidently the largest of any archive. Smaller collections are held in other National Archives branches, as well as in some Kansas county museums and historical societies.

There is no comparable collection of Missouri affidavits.

Why some survived and others did not is uncertain. The need for the affidavits ended with the armistice in November 1918. The National Archives was not established until 1934. Local authorities had been charged with registering alien enemy, and those agencies may have kept or disposed of the affidavits for various reasons.

Decades ago, the Kansas affidavits were consigned to the trash bin during the building of a new federal building in Topeka. A researcher familiar with the documents saw them and had them recovered. Because of someone's sharp eye, the documents endure, capturing in a vivid, timeless way a distant fear.

Indeed, some registrants had a subtle way of objecting to the imputation that they were an enemy.

Several elderly veterans who lived at the National Military Home in Leavenworth and who had served in the Union Army in the Civil War faced the camera wearing their uniforms. Their stripes and decorations — their loyalty — were there for all to see.

German natives who registered with local authorities in Kansas at the beginning of World War I. Among them were nuns and 70-somethings.
Record Group 118

aroline Liebsch

Max Liebsch

Amanda Ida Heine

Christina Pauler

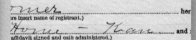

UNITED STATES OF AMERICA

Department of Justice

REGISTRATION AFFIDAVIT OF ALIEN ENEMY

sworn to in triplicate and accompanied by four unmounted photographs
ll four photographs should be signed by registrant across the face of the ph
write, he must make his mark in the signature space and affix his left th

t must be signed and sworn to before, a registration officer, who will fill
rized to administer the oath hereto to persons registering as alien enemies

_____ her__
re insert name of registrant.)

___ Home __ Kan __ and t
affidavit signed and oath administered.)

Dora Balk

Amalia Weber

DESCRIPTION OF REGISTRANT.
(To be filled in by registration officer.)

years 7 months.   Mouth medium
5   Chin   medium
1.65   Hair   t
medium   Complexion fair
blue   Face   medium
medium
ve marks none
Anna Gehring
St Francis Hospital
Wichita KS

William F A Ehart

Rebecca Ehart

ENEMY ALIENS ALL

Born in Germany, these veterans of the Civil War proudly
wore their federal uniforms when they registered.
Record Group 118

---

10. Were you registered for the selective draft? *No* (Answer "Yes" or "No.") Where? _____ (State district of registration.)

11. State all previous military or naval or other Government service. *1861 to 1865* (Here state duties, duration, and character of military or)
In U.S. Infantry
naval or other service and nation for which registrant served.)

12. Have you ever applied for naturalization in or taken out first papers of naturalization in the United States? *no* (Answer "Yes" or "No.")

If yes, state when and where _____ (Give State or Territory, city, town, or other municipality, and name of court.)

13. Have you ever been naturalized, partly or wholly, in any country other than the United States? *no* (Answer "Yes" or "No.")

If yes, state when and where and in what country _____

14. Have you ever taken an oath of allegiance to any country, State, or nation other than the United States? *no* (Answer "Yes" or "No.")

If yes, state when and where and to what country _____

○7—1100

3

...red with a consul or representative of any country other than the United

...If yes, state when and where and to whom and for what country and

No (Answer "Yes" or "No.") If yes, state when, where, and on what

Are you on parole? (Answer "Yes" or "No.")

No If yes, state number of permit. _____

...swers by me made are true.

(Signature) *Albert H. Sockland.*

Sworn to before me this *9th day of Feb*, 19*18*
at *National Military Home. Kans*

_____ (Registration officer.)

_____ (Official title, police or post office.)

Left thumb print, if registrant can not write.

DESCRIPTION OF REGISTRANT.
(To be filled in by registration officer.)

Age *72* years. Mouth *Small*
Height *5* ft. *11* in. Chin *Round*
Weight *190* Hair *Gray*
Forehead *Prominent* Complexion *Fair*
Eyes *Blue* Face *Oval*
Nose *Straight* *Short*
Distinctive marks *Wound on left side...*
Name *Albert H Sockland*
Address *Nat'l Milt Home - Kans* ○7—1100
Co K.

34 | GREAT PLAINS ORIGINALS — HISTORIC DOCUMENTS FROM AMERICA'S HEARTLAND

10. Were you registered for the selective draft? _No_ Where? _____
(Answer "Yes" or "No.")   (State district of registration.)

11. State all previous military or naval or other Government service_____
(Here state duties, duration, and character of militar
U.S. Army – 3 yrs & 3 mos. – Infantry
naval or other service and nation for which registrant served.)

15. Have you since Janu

States for military or naval or

for what service _____

12. Have you ever applied for naturalization in or taken out first papers of naturalization in the United States? _No_
(Answer "Yes" or "

If yes, state when and where_____
(Give State or Territory, city, town, or other municipality, and name of court.)

16. Have you ever been

charges?_____

13. Have you ever been naturalized, partly or wholly, in any country other than the United States? _No_
(Answer "Yes" or "No.")

If yes, state when and where and in what country_____

17. Have you a permit to

14. Have you ever taken an oath of allegiance to any country, State, or nation other than the United States? _No_
(Answer "Yes" or "N

If yes, state when and where and to what country_____

I solemnly swear that a

c 7—1100

(Signature) _Can not Write_ _____

Sworn to before me this _7th day of Feb_, 19 _18_

at _National Military Home Kans_

John T Brothers
(Registration officer.)

Postmaster
(Official title, police or post office.)

Left thumb print, if registrant can not write.

DESCRIPTION OF REGISTRANT.
(To be filled in by registration officer.)

Age _76_ years.   Mouth _Small_

Height _5_ ft. _3_ in.   Chin _Med_

Weight _100_   Hair _Gray_

Forehead _Med_   Complexion _Fair_

Eyes _Blue_   Face _Long_

Nose _Med_

Distinctive marks _Small Mustache_

Name _Henry Romer_

Address _Nat'l Mil't Home – Ks_

c 7—1100

HOME ECONOMICS GO TO WAR

Washington realized that the nation's food supply would figure crucially in the U. S. effort in World War I, and officials knew where to aim. In May 1917 Agriculture Secretary David F. Houston urged American families to practice thrift at lunch and dinner, and he addressed his appeal to "The Women of the United States."

Houston's message took a symbol of domestic drudgery — the apron — and transformed it into military apparel. Women who practiced household food conservation, Houston said, could "make of the housewife apron a uniform of national significance."

The challenge for the U.S. Food Administration, established in August 1917, was to bring the message of personal sacrifice to the streets. So a flatbed truck carrying women dressed in starched outfits traveled the streets of St. Louis promoting recipes for "War Bread," made of potatoes. Wheat, after all, was needed to feed the armed forces. The Missouri Pacific railroad stopped at towns along its lines where more women, also dressed in white, gave presentations on canning foods.

Shop-window displays told the virtues of the potato. In one such display the humble spud was draped in red, white and blue, and celebrated as a substitute for milk and flour in cakes.

The Food Administration had its own advertising arm, producing posters for outdoors and in. One familiar poster exhorted Americans to eat more corn and oats and less wheat and meat. That poster wound up in another window display in the heartland.

The stakes were high.

"Make economy fashionable," Houston said in his 1917 appeal, "lest it become obligatory."

It didn't. The war ended the next year, and the Food Administration was terminated in 1920.

Wending their way through St. Louis, above, promoters advertised ingredients and recipes that didn't compromise the war effort. Right: two such recipes.
Record Group 4

SAVORY STEW

1 lb. meat

2 tablespoons of fat
from the meat

4 medium potatoes or
1 cup of barley, rice
or hominy grits

Onions, carrots, green peas or
beans, turnips or cabbage - any
two or more of these Parsley or
soup herbs

1 teaspoon salt

$\frac{1}{2}$ teaspoon pepper

Cut the meat in small pieces, brown in the fat. Add the herbs or
parsley and the seasonings, 1$\frac{1}{2}$ quarts of water and the cereals.
Simmer for 1$\frac{1}{2}$ hours or use the fireless cooker. If potatoes are
used, cut up in small pieces and add to the stew after it has
cooked one hour. Allow an hour for the vegetables to cook if the
stew simmers, less time if it boils.

MEAT PIE

1 pound Hamburger steak
or left-over meat

1 onion

2 tablespoons fat

2 tablespoons flour

$\frac{1}{2}$ teaspoon salt

2 cups tomato

3 cups corn meal, mush
cooked rice, homany grits,
or mashed potatoes

Melt the fat, add the onion sliced and the meat. Stir until the
red color of the meat is gone, add the flour, stir until smooth,
add salt and tomatoes. Grease a baking dish, put in a layer of
cereal, add the meat and gravy and cover with the cereal. Bake

HOME ECONOMICS GO TO WAR

Make a little meat go a long way.

3 LBS. BEEF *at* .30 *Cost* .90 = 2850 Calories

1½ LBS. BEEF *at* .30 *Cost* 45 = 1425 Calories
1 LB. CARROTS " .05 210 "
1 LB. ONIONS " .05 225 "
2 LBS. POTATOES " .08½ 650 "
1 CUP RICE " .05 867 "

MEAT COST .90 = 2850 Calories   MEAT & VEGETABLES *Cost* .66½ = 3377 Calories

Extend your meat with vegetables. Gain money and variety.

The Road to Victory

Hash Meat Pie
Goulash Croquettes
Stew

From shop windows in Nebraska to whistle stops across Missouri, the U.S. Food Administration commissioned campaigns to conserve food, left and above. Right: patriotic glories of the potato.

Record Group 4

VIGILANTE JUSTICE

To most, tarring and feathering was a form of rough justice practiced on the 19th-century American frontier. Some vigilantes, however, revived it during World War I.

After the United States declared war on Germany in April 1917, the Department of Justice asked citizens to report behavior they deemed suspicious. Some people responded by forming groups with names such as the Boy Spies of America. One unfortunate target was John Meintz, a German-American who lived in Minnesota.

Meintz had joined an agrarian organization that some Minnesota officials considered disloyal. In the charged political climate of the time, a mob attacked Meintz, tarring and feathering him.

A photographer documented the abuse he received at the hands of the vigilantes. Meintz brought his grievances to federal court, but he lost.

After vigilantes were finished with him, John Meintz showed what a tarring-and-feathering looked like.
Record Group 21

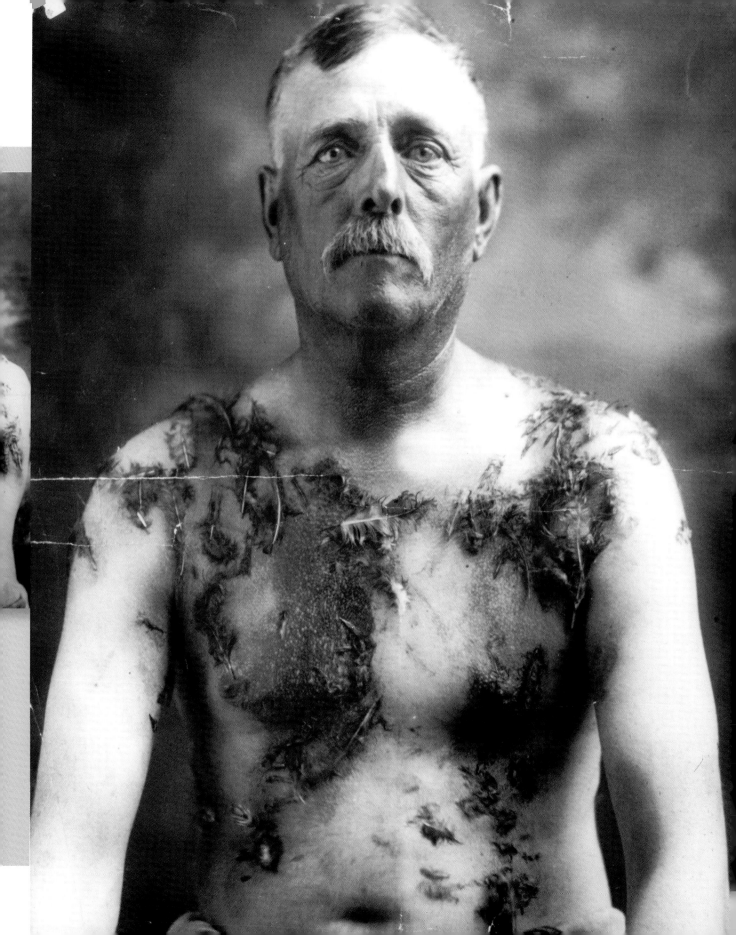

DANGEROUS OPINION

The mugshots of Carl Gleeser and Jacob Frohwerk offered no hints how they differed from most other prisoners of the U.S. Penitentiary in Leavenworth. But their daily labor records did: Both worked in the prison printing office, and among Gleeser's possessions when he arrived at the prison on April 30, 1918, were a pencil and notebook.

The two men's crime: distributing dangerous opinion.

Both were newspapermen. Both were American citizens. Gleeser had lived in the United States for 46 years, Frohwerk for 37. Both were arrested in Kansas City in January 1918, charged with violations of the Espionage Act of 1917, which criminalized "false reports or false statements with intent to interfere" with military matters or to promote the enemy's success. They were natives of Germany, against which the United States had declared war the previous April.

Gleeser, 62, owned a German-language weekly, the *Missouri Staats Zeitung*, published in Kansas City with a circulation of barely 1,000. Frohwerk, 54, wrote editorials for it and sold advertising.

Gleeser pleaded not guilty, then changed his plea to guilty and got five years. Frohwerk's case went to trial. His 88-page indictment included editorials and other articles published in the newspaper from June to December 1917. Some articles questioned the war motives of the United States. One editorial described the country's defense contracts as "paid out of the sweat and blood of the American people. That's why we are in this war."

Part of Frohwerk's defense was that the government had no evidence the newspaper had printed falsehoods, a provision of the Espionage Act. Also, Frohwerk argued that the First Amendment made the act unconstitutional, anyway. He got 10 years.

From Leavenworth, Frohwerk appealed but in 1919 the U.S. Supreme Court unanimously upheld the ruling. Today Frohwerk's name lives on in legal circles; *Frohwerk v. United States* often is cited to show how the thinking of Justice Oliver Wendell Holmes Jr. evolved on free-speech and free-press matters.

The comparatively small audience that the Kansas City newspaper reached gave Holmes no comfort.

"The circulation of the paper was in quarters where a little breath would be enough to kindle a flame," Holmes wrote in an opinion summarizing the court's thinking. Not until the mid-1920s, some legal scholars believe, did Holmes increase his regard for First Amendment protections.

Meanwhile, the war ended in November 1918, and so did imprisonment of Frohwerk and Gleeser. The sentences of both were commuted in 1919.

When Frohwerk walked out of Leavenworth in January 1920, a reporter for *The Kansas City Star* was present, and wrote, "He is a greatly changed man."

Or maybe not.

"It is alleged that I wrote articles that was a violation of the Espionage Act," Frohwerk declared on a trusty prisoner's agreement, which granted him certain special privileges. "I plead guilty."

Carl Gleeser, top, and Jacob Frohwerk in their Leavenworth mugshots. Among Frohwerk's visitors was a William Volker. The name matched that of a wealthy Kansas City merchant and philanthropist.
Record Group 129

Grade...
Other Names..
....
No's of same name..............................
Special Permits....................................

UNITED STATE[S]
LEAVENWO[RTH]

NAME........ Jacob[...]

	CORRESPONDENT	Relative	POST OFFICE	STATE	JAN.
Rec'd		Wife	Kansas City	Kans	
Sent			2317 No 11th St	✓	
Rec'd	Carl Alberts	Fr.	Helmond	Holland	
[Se]nt					
[Rec]'d	Keplinger + Tucket	atty	Kansas City	Mo	
[Se]nt	Franz E. Lindquist	atty	Kansas City	Mo	
[Se]nt	A. A. Kitterer	Fr.	Kansas City	Mo	
[Rec]'d	Rev. John Sauer	fr.	Kansas City	Mo.	
			5018 Euclid Ave		
	Edward C. Little	Rep.	Washington	DC	
[Re]c'd	Albert Ladzinski	fr	Kansas City	Mo	
[Re]c'd	L. Bender	fr.	Kansas City	Mo	
Rec'd	William Volker	fr.	Kansas City	Mo.	
	Daniel Stumpp	fr.	Kansas City	Kans.	
	Mr. & Mrs. Geo. Gasthin	Bro Sis	Los Angeles	Calif	
			1788 W. 24 st		
	Mr & Mrs Wm Frohwerk	Bro Sis	West Berkely	Calif	
			1200 Stanage Ave		
[Re]c'd	J. B. Hipple	fr.	Kansas City	Kans.	
			K. C. Press		
	Henry Oberman	fr	Kansas City	Mo.	
			11th + Mc Gee st		
	Marie Rhein	Fr.	Reading	Pa	
Sent					
Rec'd					

UNITED STATES PENITENTIARY

LEAVENWORTH, KANSAS

RECORD OF   Carl Gleeser   No. 12644
Alias   Color   White
Crime   Violation of Espionage Act   Military or Civil   Civil
2-2- yr and 1-lyr sentences cumulative and 10-1 yr sentences concurrent with 1st 1yr sente[nce]
Sentence 5   years, --   months, --   days.
Fine   ---   Cost   Costs
Received at Penitentiary   April 30, 1918   From W. D. Missouri, Kansas City
Date of Sentence   April, 29, 1918   Sentence Begins   April 30, 1918
Maximum term ends   April 29, 1923   Minimum term ends   January 4, 1922
Good time allowed, 480   days. Occupation,   Newspaper Work   Age, 62 years
Eligible to parole   December 29, 1919

COMMUTATION.
May 8th. 1919.

Official papers commuted Frohwerk's and Gleeser's sentences. Above right: Frohwerk announced his homecoming.

Record Group 129

Department of Justice,
July 9, 1919
Washington, ~~May 7th~~ 19

To The Warden,
U.S. Penitentiary,
Leavenworth, Kaus.

Sir:

Herewith receive Warrant for commutation
sentence of Jacob Frohwerk,

which please deliver to *him* and report RELEASE at
time to this Department, retaining this letter as your autho

By direction of the Attorney General.

Very respectfully,

Robert H. Lurm
Assistant Pardon

[OVER.]

Department of Justice,
Washington, May 8th 1919

To The Warden,
U.S. Penitentiary,
Leavenworth, Kaus.

Sir:

Herewith receive Warrant for commutation of
sentence of Carl Gleeser,

which please deliver to *him* and report RELEASE at proper
time to this Department, retaining this letter as your authority.

By direction of the Attorney General.

Very respectfully,

James A. Finch
Pardon Attorney.

Commuted to One Year
and One Day.
[OVER.]

═══ DO NOT WRITE ABOVE THIS LINE ═══

NO. A 00756   Jan.7,1920.   19

Warden, U. S. Penitentiary:

   I respectfully request permission to send the following telegram, the cost to be charged to my account.

        Name _____ **Frohwerk** _____   Reg. No. __ **14036**

Mrs.Jacob Frohwerk,
2317 North 11th Street,
Kansas City,Kansas.

            Coming home. Probably Friday. I have

everything needed.

                              Papa.

Permitted: _____

                    Warden

33-422

WOODROW WILSON,

President of the United States of America,

To all to whom these presents shall come, Greeting:

Whereas

        Jacob Frohwerk was convicted in the United States
District Court for the Western District of Missouri of violating Section 3, Title I, of the Espionage Act of June 15, 1917, and on June
twenty-ninth, 1918, was sentenced to imprisonment for ten years in the
United States Penitentiary at Leavenworth, Kansas, and to pay a fine
of five hundred dollars and costs; and,

        Whereas an appeal was taken to the Supreme Court, which court
affirmed the judgment; and,

        Whereas it has been made to appear to me that the said Jacob
Frohwerk is a fit object of executive clemency:————————

        *In testimony whereof I have hereunto signed
my name and caused the seal of the Department of
Justice to be affixed.*

        *Done at the District of Columbia this Seventeenth
day of   June   in the year of our Lord
One Thousand Nine Hundred and   Nineteen   and
of the Independence of the United States the One Hundred
and Forty-Third.*

                              Woodrow Wilson

By the President:
A. Mitchell Palmer
        Attorney General.

We, the jury, find the defendant Rose Pastor Stokes _____ guilty as charged in the first count of the indictment herein.

Warner W. Caton
Foreman.

'I AM NOT FOR THE GOVERNMENT'

The price of speaking your mind rises and falls with the climate of the times. Once the United States entered World War I, the price rose dramatically, and Rose Pastor Stokes paid dearly.

Stokes, an anti-war activist, wrote a letter to the editor of *The Kansas City Star* in March 1918 and wound up sentenced to 10 years in prison.

The Star covered a speech Stokes gave to a Kansas City women's club, but the account was not to her satisfaction. So she wrote these words, which appeared in *The Star's* morning edition, *The Kansas City Times:*

"A headline in this evening's issue of *The Star* reads: 'Mrs. Stokes for Government and Against War at the Same Time.' I am not for the government. In the interview that follows I am quoted as having said, 'I believe the government of the United States should have the unqualified support of every citizen in its war aims.'

"I made no such statement, and I believe no such thing. No government which is for the profiteers can also be for the people, and I am for the people, while the government is for the profiteers."

Because about 3,000 free copies of *The Times* containing that letter were distributed to area military camps, Stokes was accused of trying to undermine the war effort. A grand jury indicted her on three counts of violating the Espionage Act. A jury found her guilty on all three counts.

Stokes became one of 877 people found guilty out of 1,956 prosecuted under the Espionage Act, and a judge sentenced her to 10 years.

In 1920, after the war was over, a federal appeals court overturned the verdict.

Charges, testimony and jury's verdict in the case of Rose Pastor Stokes.
Record Group 21

The Presid

O THE MARSHA
DISTRICT
AND TO H

WHEREAS, ...
in writing under oath
the..... *Wee*
Division charging tha
.....
late of...... *Jo*
did, on or about the.
A. D. 19*18*., at.
Section 3 of Title
Revised Statutes of
oneously
and false
with the of
and proce
to procu
the United
feloneously
insubordi
refusal of du
forces of

contrary to the form
peace and dignity of
NOW, THEREFORE,
United States of Am

of the United States of Ameri

HE UNITED STATES FOR THE *Wester*
Missouri

PUTIES, OR ANY OR EITHER OF THEM:

....Schmitz .... has made co

me, the undersigned, a United States Commission

....District of .. *Missou* ³ˢ

Rose Pastor Stok

.... County, in the State of ..

20ᵗʰ ....day of.. *leo*

...City in said District, in vio

Act of Congress Approved

ted States, unlawfully *will full*

...and convey fal

....ments with intent

ion) and success of

...s of the United St

the success of the e

, and unlawfully, w

...e and attempt to

...n, disloyalty, mut

...in the military an

...United States

atute in such cases made and provided

ited States of America.

E HEREBY COMMANDED, in the name of the Presiden

apprehend the said *...*

Pastor Stokes

Cross - examination

BY MR. SILVERS.

1
2
3
   Q Mrs. Stokes, I understand you to say that you are a
4 socialist?   A I am.
5   Q How long, Mrs. Stokes, have you been a socialist?
6   A All my life.
7   Q You are also what you term an internationalist?
8   A I believe in the international solidarity of the people.
9   Q You are what you call an internationalist or international?
10 I am not asking you to explain or state whether or not you also
11 those views which would constitute an international.
12   MR. STEDMAN: International or internationalist?
13   MR. SILVERS: Internationalist; I think I used that
14 term in the first place.
15   MR. STEDMAN: You dropped your voice; I did not hear
16   you.
17 (No answer)
18   Q Mrs. Stokes, when did you first affiliate yourself formally
19 with the socialist party?   A I affiliated myself formally
20 with the socialist party years ago in Cleveland.
21   Q In Cleveland, Ohio?   A Yes.
22   Q That was years ago?   A Yes, I was a very young girl.
23 I can tell you, if you wish to know the period.
24   Q I do not care to know anything about the period, but I am
25 asking you if you can give me the date.   A I can give you
26 the approximate time.
27   Q You said it was years ago when you were a girl in Cleveland?
28   A Yes.
29   Q Mrs. Stokes, you continued as a member of the socialist
30 party up until what time?   A I drifted out of the party in

WAR AND ITS OFFSPRING | 47

A REFORMIST LIFE

Kate Richards O'Hare fit the profile of the progressive reformer.

For one thing, Carrie Katherine Richards and her family had known true adversity. Her parents — who were homesteading near Ada, Kansas, when she was born — faced bankruptcy and moved to the slums of Kansas City in 1887. For another, she had been active in politics from early on. As a teacher in Nebraska, she contributed articles to a nearby Populist newspaper. And she knew the realities of manual labor. After moving back to Kansas City she became an apprentice machinist and joined the machinists union.

She had devoted time to the temperance movement, but gradually grew skeptical of that brand of reform.

Upon hearing Mary Harris "Mother" Jones speak at a Kansas City union hall, she began studying socialism. From the turn of the 20th century, Americans knew her as one of the more outspoken advocates of socialism in the country.

Living in Girard, Kansas, home of the socialist newspaper *Appeal to Reason,* she met Frank O'Hare and married him in 1902. They spent their honeymoon organizing socialist meetings, and together founded a publication called *National Rip-Saw,* which they later renamed *Social Revolution.* In 1910 she ran for Congress on the socialist ticket in Kansas. By 1917 she was traveling the country delivering speeches opposing the Unites States' involvement in the war.

That July, after making an address in Bowman, North Dakota, O'Hare was indicted for sedition. An amendment to the Espionage Act, approved the previous year, outlawed speaking, writing or publishing anything that undermined the interests of the federal government.

A judge sentenced her to five years. An appeals court upheld the ruling and the U.S. Supreme Court declined to review it. She entered the Missouri state penitentiary in 1919. Her sentence was commuted in 1920, and President Calvin Coolidge later granted her a full pardon.

Her time behind bars in Jefferson City changed O'Hare. By the mid-1920s she was devoting most of her energy to prison reform.

In her testimony, O'Hare answered questions about her talk at Bowman, South Dakota, including references to spilled American blood and the roles of European women.
Record Group 21

Q In the delivery of this lecture at Bowman, North Dakota, on or about the month of July, 1917, did you have any
purpose or intent to interfere with, or obstruct in any way
the enlistment service of the United States?   A I did not.

Q Did you at that time have or harbor any intent or
purpose to obstruct or hinder the recruiting service of the
United States? A May I ask if you mean the Conscription
Law?

Q The two terms are used in the Concsription Law, recruiting and enlisting?   A I had no intention of interfer-
ing with either the enlistment or the recruiting, either one.

Q It is charged in the indictment in this case, Mrs.
O'Hare, that you, at the City of Bowman, in the County of
Bowman, in a public speech on or about the 17th day of July,
stated in the presence of 125 people in substance that any person who enlisted in the army of the United States for service
in France would be used for fertilizer, and that was all he
was good for. I will ask you to state whether you made that
statement, or that in substance, in that lecture?   A Most
emphatically I did not.

Q What, according to your recollection, is the statement
that this allegation is distorted into that you made at that
lecture?   A As near as I can judge, the statement that has
been distorted into that allegation is this: I said, "Please
understand me, and do not misquote me and say I am opposed
to enlistment. I am not. If any young man feels it is his
duty to enlist in the army of the United States then he should
enlist, and God bless him." I said, "His blood may enrich" –

or possibly fertilize, speaking to farmers, - "His blood may enrich the soil of France." Then I stopped and questioned, - "Perhaps that may be the best use for it?" But that was a question. That is the statement, so far as I can imagine, or I can judge, that has been distorted into this charge.

Q Up to that time, to your knowledge, were any of the American soldiers engaged in fighting in France, so far as you remember, at that time? Do you remember?   A No, I don't think there were any American soldiers in France at that time, to the best of my knowledge.

Q What have you to say in regard to the statements attributed to you by some of the witnesses for the government, and charged in the indictment to have been made by you in regard to the women of this country as brood sows. What, if anything, did you say in that connection?   A The statement that in my judgment has been distorted into the allegation was this: When the governments and churches of the European countries demanded of the women of Europe that they should give themselves to the soldiers going away to war, in marriage or out, in order that those soldiers might breed before they died,- that when the church and government demanded that of women, they reduced them to the status of breeding animals, or brood sows on a stock farm.

Q By either of these statements which you have corrected and testified that you used in that lecture, containing the word "fertilizer," and the words "brood sows" or "breeding animals," - did you intend by them, or either of them, to in any way obstruct the recruiting or enlistment in the service

Q And you belong to the International Union?

A I belong to the International Bureau.

Q And have been in touch with the International Union since war was declared? A I have been in touch with the allies, the socialists in the allied nations since war was declared.

Q And had a letter from one in England a short time ago?

A I did.

Q On the evening in question, at Bowman, you told the people there you were opposed to war? A I told the people in Bowman that I abhorred war.

Q You urged on the young men the enlistment at Bowman?

A I told the young men that if they felt it their duty to enlist to do so, and God bless them.

Q You used that language in connection with your lecture with the idea that you were asking the Creator to bless the young men in the war? A Most assuredly, in the most reverent terms.

Q Were you just as reverent with reference to the statement when you mentioned the fact that the blood of these young men might become fertilizer upon the soil of France? A I was.

Q Do you believe that? A Do I believe what?

Q That the blood of the young men over there may become a fertilizer to the soil of France, or Belgium, or Germany?

A I do.

Q And when you got down to the point where you desired to

Later in her testimony, O'Hare discussed her international contacts and the degree of reverence she used in her speech in South Dakota.
Record Group 21

CLEARING THE GROUND

The Great Plains, with its expanses of barely populated land, provided excellent sites for ordnance plants. There, the shells and explosives used to fight the Axis in World War II would be produced. Typically, the government and its contractors looked for open acreage far enough from habitation in case of an accident, yet near enough to towns and cities to provide a work force. They paid farmers for their land and structures and moved or destroyed homes, barns, sheds and other farm buildings. Sometimes, the process was recorded in photographs.

These snapshots were meant to show the buildings being displaced by the Des Moines, Iowa, ordnance works. They also documented the passing of a rural life, and evidently caught some of the people who were moving out. In each shot, a boy or a girl, a young man and or an old man — possibly owners and residents — held small boards enumerating the property.

Outside a barn, a house and a shed, an unidentified Iowa boy — probably a resident of the area — held a sign numbering each structure that would make way for the ordnance plant.
Record Group 270

CLEARING THE GROUND

A girl, young man and older men — area residents all? — stood outside various buildings being destroyed or moved.
Record Group 270

WORRIES AT AN ORDNANCE PLANT

CONFIDE

Munitions plant operators had to prepare for any eventuality in World War II. The country was at war, and nothing could be assumed — even in Iowa, far from either coast.

So in 1943 a member of the Seventh Army Service Command drew up a contingency plan for hostilities at the Des Moines Ordnance Plant. The plan centered not on a foreign enemy but evidently on the 600 or so African-American employees of the plant — and on the white employees and other residents apparently upset by the presence of the black workers.

A six-page memo detailed the "standard operations procedures for racial disturbances." There had been no significant hostilities between white and black Iowans, the unnamed author conceded, but there remained a problem of "racial consciousness."

The author pointed to the "militant aggressiveness" of some African-Americans in striving "to attain social and economic equality." Another issue was the presence in uniform of black members of the Women's Army Corps. The duties of the Seventh Army Service Command included training and assigning new WACs.

"The conduct of the WACs is not seriously criticized," the author wrote, "but by their numbers on the street the racial problem is more brought to mind."

The author considered the worst case, citing the number of available men in the Des Moines Police Department, which was 195; the number of its patrol and scout cars, which was 29, and its three submachine guns, eight rifles and 14 shotguns. Also listed were the numbers of the Iowa State Guard ("Morale is high") and some deficiencies, such as its lack of motor transportation. If federal troops were needed, the memo says where they could be housed.

Plant operators were urged to place guards to prevent clashes between white and African-American employees. Also, the head of the WAC training center in Des Moines was asked to restrict the movement of black WACs on city streets.

Five years later, President Harry Truman issued Executive Order 9981, which began integration of the U.S. armed forces.

The Des Moines Ordnance Plant and a page from its emergency plan.
Record Group 156 (memorandum) and 270 (aerial photograph)

TIAL

CONFIDENTIAL

DES MOINES IOWA PLAN
SOP to EPW
Part I.

ESTIMATE OF THE SITUATION

1. <u>DISTRICT ESTIMATE</u> - It is not anticipated that racial disorders of serious importance would occur in the State of Iowa except in Des Moines and vicinity and possibly Waterloo. Of the total Negro population of the state (16,694, Bureau of Census 1940) 1498 live in Waterloo and 6360 in Des Moines; the latter figure is believed to have increased somewhat in the past two years.

There is nothing serious in the situation at present in either community, and any probability of trouble in Waterloo is considered remote. The situation in Des Moines could quickly become serious, and should be closely watched. There is no evidence of subversive leadership or of disloyalty, although that possibility should not be overlooked. The problem is at present one of racial consciousness, and increasing dislike between whites and colored. It is increased by the militant aggressiveness of certain Negroes in the fight to at this time attain social and economic equality. There is no doubt that white resentment is increased somewhat by the presence in the city of the
of Negro WACs. The conduct of the WACs is not seriously
t by their numbers on the streets in uniform the racial
ught more to mind.

vent of trouble, the situation will not be particularly
he coal mines in the vicinity and the war production
o exceptions employ only a few. Iowa Packing Company
130 out of a total of 1230. Des Moines Ordnance Plant
imately 600 out of a total of 17,400.

e are three principal Negro residential district center-

and Center Streets.

17th and Walker.

area in Southeast Des Moines known as Precinct 50.

the first named is in close proximity to the business
city.

ES AVAILABLE TO CIVIL AUTHORITIES

POLICE FORCE - The Des Moines Police Department consists
addition, the county sheriff has 48 deputies. Combined,
trol and scout cars, all equipped with radio receivers,
guns, 8 rifles, 14 shotguns, 2 gas guns and a sufficient
ition.

STATE GUARD - The Iowa State Guard consists of a Head-
iy, Supply Company, two infantry regiments, each with

- 1 -

GREETINGS! WELL, NOT REALLY

Five months into World War II, middle-aged men reported to their draft boards.

Over three days in April 1942, all men 45 to 64 years old were required to register with the Selective Service.

The idea was to conduct a manpower census so the federal government could know how many mature men could be found, and what skills could be put to use if needed. After registering, the men received three-page occupational questionnaires.

The first Selective Service registration occurred in October 1940 for men 21 to 35. A second came on July 1, 1941, for men who had reached 21 since the first registration. A third in February 1942 included men 35 to 44.

That April, middle-aged men had their turn. Even U.S. senators took part. Among them was 58-year-old Harry S. Truman. Also registering was Truman's 56-year-old brother, John Vivian Truman, who worked for the Federal Housing Administration in Kansas City.

Psychiatrists signed up — men such as 48-year-old Karl Menninger, a founder of the Menninger Clinic in Topeka. So did retired major-league baseball stars such as Grover Cleveland Alexander, 55, and former Negro Leagues stars such as Wilbur "Bullet Joe" Rogan, 52.

Today, tens of thousands of four-inch by six-inch registration cards from all over Missouri, Kansas, Nebraska, Iowa, Minnesota and the Dakotas survive in the files of the Central Plains Region. Genealogists regard the cards as a reliable federal footprint for the whereabouts of ancestors in April 1942.

Baseball historians have used them to find where ballplayers lived after their playing careers ended — not to mention capturing authentic autographs.

Grover Cleveland Alexander, who pitched his last major league game in 1930, was by 1942 living in Grand Island, Nebraska. That was not far from Elba, Nebraska, where he was born in 1887, and St. Paul, Nebraska, where he would die eight years later.

Rogan lived in Kansas City, where he had played 11 seasons for the Kansas City Monarchs, the last in 1930. His registration card listed his employer as the city's main post office. It listed no home telephone number.

ARD—(Men born on or after April 28, 1877 and on or before February 16, 1897)

1. NAME (Print)			ORDER NUMBER
Harry-	S	Truman	—
(First)	(Middle)	(Last)	

CE (Print)

Deleware, Independence Jackson, Mo.

nd street)   (Town, township, village, or city)   (County)   (State)

CE OF RESIDENCE GIVEN ON THE LINE ABOVE WILL DETERMINE LOCAL BOARD
RISDICTION; LINE 2 OF REGISTRATION CERTIFICATE WILL BE IDENTICAL]

S

ate Office Building, Washington, D. C

[Mailing address if other than place indicated on line 2. If same insert word same]

O	5. AGE IN YEARS	6. PLACE OF BIRTH
	58	Lamar, Mo
	DATE OF BIRTH	(Town or county)
	May 8, 1884	
(Number)	(Mo.) (Day) (Yr.)	(State or country)

SS OF PERSON WHO WILL ALWAYS KNOW YOUR ADDRESS

s W. Truman   219 No. Deleware, Independence, Mc
                                 Jackson, Mo.

E AND ADDRESS

United States Senate

MENT OR BUSINESS

Washington, D. C

nd street or R.F.D. number)   (Town)   (County)   (State)

I HAVE VERIFIED ABOVE ANSWERS AND THAT THEY ARE TRUE.

16—21630-2

Harry Truman

(Registrant's signature)

SERIAL NUMBER	NAME (Print)			ORDER NUMBER
U 424	John Vivian		Truman	
	(First)	(Middle)	(Last)	

2. PLACE OF RESIDENCE (Print)

Grand View, Missouri   Jackson #1

(Number and street) (Town, township, village, or city) (County) (State)

[THE PLACE OF RESIDENCE GIVEN ON THE LINE ABOVE WILL DETERMINE LOCAL BOARD
JURISDICTION; LINE 2 OF REGISTRATION CERTIFICATE WILL BE IDENTICAL]

3. MAILING ADDRESS

Grand View, Missouri   Jackson co.

[Mailing address if other than place indicated on line 2. If same insert word same]

4. TELEPHONE	5. AGE IN YEARS	6. PLACE OF BIRTH
Kansas City,	56	Belton
	DATE OF BIRTH	(Town or county)
Dwight 5533	April 25, 1886	Missouri
(Exchange) (Number)	(Mo.) (Day) (Yr.)	(State or country)

7. NAME AND ADDRESS OF PERSON WHO WILL ALWAYS KNOW YOUR ADDRESS

Mrs. Luella Truman Grand View, Missouri

8. EMPLOYER'S NAME AND ADDRESS

Federal Housing Administration 301 Federal Courts Bdg.   Kansas City Mo.

9. PLACE OF EMPLOYMENT OR BUSINESS

Same

(Number and street or R.F.D. number) (Town) (County) (State)

I AFFIRM THAT I HAVE VERIFIED ABOVE ANSWERS AND THAT THEY ARE TRUE.

D.S.S. Form 1   (over)   16—21630-2   *J. Vivian Truman*
(Revised 4-1-42)   (Registrant's signature)

Brothers Harry and Vivian Truman, both in their 50s, registered with Selective Service.
Record Group 147

REGISTRATION CARD—(Men born on or after April 28, 1877 and on or before February 16, 1897)

SERIAL NUMBER
U **981**

1. NAME (Print)
George (First)   Harold (Middle)   Sisler (Last)

ORDER NUMBER

2. PLACE OF RESIDENCE (Print)
6343 Pershing (Number and street)   University City (Town, township, village, or city)   St. Louis County, Missouri (County) (State)

[THE PLACE OF RESIDENCE GIVEN ON THE LINE ABOVE WILL DETERMINE LOCAL BOARD JURISDICTION; LINE 2 OF REGISTRATION CERTIFICATE WILL BE IDENTICAL]

3. MAILING ADDRESS
Same [Mailing address if other than place indicated on line 2. If same insert word same]

4. TELEPHONE
Pa 7713 (Exchange) (Number)

5. AGE IN YEARS
49

DATE OF BIRTH
Mar 24 1893 (Mo.) (Day) (Yr.)

6. PLACE OF BIRTH
Nimisclay, (Town or county)
Ohio (State or country)

7. NAME AND ADDRESS OF PERSON WHO WILL ALWAYS KNOW YOUR ADDRESS
Geo H Sisler, Jr. Albany, Ga

8. EMPLOYER'S NAME AND ADDRESS
Sisler-Hummel Sporting Goods Co, 1114 Locust St St Louis, Mo.

9. PLACE OF EMPLOYMENT OR BUSINESS
1114 Locust St St Louis Mo. (Number and street or R.F.D. number) (Town) (County) (State)

I AFFIRM THAT I HAVE VERIFIED ABOVE ANSWERS AND THAT THEY ARE TRUE
Geo H Sisler (Registrant's signature)

D. S. S. Form 1
(Revised 4-1-42) (over) 16—21630-2

REGISTRATION

SERIAL NUMBER
U 2466

2 PLACE OF RESI
1836
(Numb
[THE PL

3. MAILING ADD

4. TELEPHONE
NO
(Exchange)

7. NAME AND ADI
MRS CARI

8. EMPLOYER'S N

9. PLACE OF EMP
(Numb

I AFFIRM TH

D. S. S. Form
(Revised 4-1-42)

Major-leaguers George Sisler and Grover Cleveland Alexander and Negro Leagues star Wilbur "Bullet Joe" Rogan registered.

Record Group 147

(Men born on or after April 28, 1877 and on or before February 16, 1897)

AME (Print)   ORDER NUMBER

OVER   CLEVLAND   ALEXANDER.

(First)   (Middle)   (Last)

nt)

TH HUSTON GRAND ISLAND HALL-NE

(Town, township, village, or city)   (County)   (State)

RESIDENCE GIVEN ON THE LINE ABOVE WILL DETERMINE LOCAL BOARD
TION; LINE 2 OF REGISTRATION CERTIFICATE WILL BE IDENTICAL]

E

Mailing address if other than place indicated on line 2. If same insert word same]

	5. AGE IN YEARS	6. PLACE OF BIRTH
	5 5	HOWARD CO
	DATE OF BIRTH	(Town or county)
	Feb 26 1887	NEBR.
mber)	(Mo.) (Day) (Yr.)	(State or country)

RSON WHO WILL ALWAYS KNOW YOUR ADDRESS

IST 1836 NORTH HUSTON GRAND ISLAND

DDRESS

NONE

BUSINESS

or R.F.D. number)   (Town)   (County)   (State)

VERIFIED ABOVE ANSWERS AND THAT THEY ARE TRUE.

Grover C Alexander

(over)   16—2163

REGISTRATION CARD—(Men born on or after April 28, 1877 and on or before February 16, 1897)

SERIAL NUMBER	1. NAME (Print)	ORDER NUMBER
U 2165	Wilbur (none) Rogan	
	(First) (Middle) (Last)	

2 PLACE OF RESIDENCE (Print)

2516 Harrison. K.C. Jackson – Mo.

(Number and street)   (Town, township, village, or city)   (County)   (State)

[THE PLACE OF RESIDENCE GIVEN ON THE LINE ABOVE WILL DETERMINE LOCAL BOARD
JURISDICTION; LINE 2 OF REGISTRATION CERTIFICATE WILL BE IDENTICAL]

3. MAILING ADDRESS

same

[Mailing address if other than place indicated on line 2. If same insert word same]

4. TELEPHONE	5. AGE IN YEARS	6. PLACE OF BIRTH
none	52	Oklahoma City
	DATE OF BIRTH	(Town or county)
	July 28 1889	Okla.
(Exchange) (Number)	(Mo.) (Day) (Yr.)	(State or country)

7. NAME AND ADDRESS OF PERSON WHO WILL ALWAYS KNOW YOUR ADDRESS

Beatrice Moppins – 1132 Freeman K.C. Kans

8. EMPLOYER'S NAME AND ADDRESS

General Post Office

9. PLACE OF EMPLOYMENT OR BUSINESS

General Post Office

(Number and street or R.F.D. number)   (Town)   (County)   (State)

I AFFIRM THAT I HAVE VERIFIED ABOVE ANSWERS AND THAT THEY ARE TRUE.

Wilbur Rogan.

D. S. S. Form 1   (over)   16—21630-2   (Registrant's signature)
(Revised 4-1-42)

ROSIE THE BOMB-MAKER

In the course of World War II, more than three million women worked in arms plants across the country. One of those was the Cornhusker Ordnance Plant in Grand Island, Nebraska, where bombs and artillery shells were built. More than half of Cornhusker's production employees were women.

Among their tasks were placing metal bands on shells, inserting dynamite or spray-painting bomb casings.

Making bombs and ammunition was hazardous. Out of wartime necessity — many men had joined the services — it became women's work.

Pictures of the plant documented social aspects of employment. One showed a worker in her room in the girls' dormitory; another showed an employee dance.

For the first anniversary of the plant in November 1943 an open house drew about 6,000 visitors. The plant chef baked a cake topped with a red, white and blue bomb. In it was placed a burning candle.

Explosive mixture made for delicate work at the Cornhusker Ordnance Plant.
Record Group 156

2.

ROSIE THE BOMB-MAKER

"Women Ordnance Workers ...They're WOWs!" read a sign over a conference table at the Cornhusker Ordnance Plant. For the touring photographer, at least, employees flashed smiles in the course of the potentially hazardous work of loading and capping shells and bombs.
Record Group 156

The image ticket reads:

The
CORNHUSKER
ORDNANCE ★ PLANT
THE Q. O. ORDNANCE CORPORATION
OPERATORS
Welcomes the bearer to the
1ST
Anniversary
OPEN
HOUSE
CELEBRATION
November 14, 1943

Myron Avdonah
GEN. MGR. Q.O. ORD. CORP.

LT. COL. ORD. DEPT. COMMANDING

DO NOT DETACH
★ THIS TICKET ENTITLES GUEST TO
ONE BUS TOUR OF THE PLANT AREA

NAME
ADDRESS

ARE YOU INTERESTED IN A JOB AT THIS
PLANT ?   ☐ YES   ☐ NO

NO.   06801

BAD FOR THE GIs

Just as in World War I, federal authorities during the second world war prosecuted citizens for sedition.

One of those was Elmer Garner, editor of *Publicity*, a newspaper published in Wichita, Kansas. In the 1940s Garner faced federal charges of conspiring to cause insubordination in the armed forces.

There was a difference between Garner and those individuals prosecuted under sedition laws in World War I, such as Rose Pastor Stokes and Kate Richards O'Hare.

Stokes and O'Hare clearly stood on the political left. O'Hare had been a well-known socialist since the early 1900s. Garner was on the other end of the spectrum. Scholars considered him an example of the American radical right, which perceived a Jewish influence on American politics and blamed it for the country's involvement in World War II. Garner, an elderly man in the 1940s, died during the litigation.

IN THE DISTRICT COURT OF THE UNITED STATES
FOR THE DISTRICT OF COLUMBIA.

Date April 16, 17, 1942

United States of America

v.   Criminal No.

GEORGE SYLVESTER VIERECK, ET AL

Transcript of Proceedings
TESTIMONY OF ELMER J. GARNER

Pages: 4269   4341
          4458   to   4469

Copy for

WARD & PAUL

NATIONAL { 4266
         { 4267
         { 4268

OFFICIAL REPORTERS
1762 PENNSYLVANIA AVE., N. W.
WASHINGTON, D. C.

Q   No.
be Life Magazin
ti on."   "I sai
Jewish filth t
week." Now, y

the statement in the paper that it

ile that?   A   Well, just

picture represents a representation

occasion of that kind.

ey:

his issue of your paper of March 12,

to yo

ad on

ther

azine

ypica

Week

s pro

e, Mr

ograp

That

says, "This time the

the weekly pornogr

re referring to Lif

esentative of Life

ay "This time the Jewish Front will

weekly pornographic publica-

rnographic" because of the typical

ks through its pages from week to

referring to Life Magazine, weren't

2.

Elmer Garner's newspaper, *Publicity*, questioned U.S. entry
into World War II.
Record Group 118

SAD SOUVENIRS OF THE FALLEN

In February 1942, the Army directed commanding generals to ship personal belongings of soldiers killed in the war to the quartermaster depot in Kansas City for "final disposition."

The depot was one of 25 in the United States, but its Effects Bureau was the only place where the Army processed these items in World War II. The Army had operated a similar bureau in Hoboken, New Jersey, in World War I.

Soon the bureau began receiving foreign currency, clothing, letters, cameras, wallets and, inevitably, photographs of girlfriends or wives left behind.

Though the items seemed routine, the 900 people employed by the bureau through the war were instructed never to underestimate their importance.

"To the owners they cannot be replaced," Col. John R. Murphy, effects quartermaster, told *The Kansas City Star* in 1945, "and it is this thought that is constantly in the minds of the employees of the Army Effects bureau as they carry on their work."

The processing was not for just anyone.

"Carefully selected mature women, most of whom have close relatives in the service, do this work, which results in the property, securely packed, shipped to the proper person," *The Star's* account said.

Each week, the bureau converted foreign currency at prevailing rates and shipped the money home to families. Also each week the Effects Bureau submitted written summaries of its work. The report for Sept. 24 through Sept. 30, 1944, noted that the bureau had shipped 2,695 sets of effects. That was a busy season. Soldiers taking part in the June 1944 invasion of France shipped excess effects from England to the Kansas City bureau.

From Aug. 5 through Sept. 4, 1944, bureau personnel shipped nearly 10,000 packages to designated addressees.

Memos also reported the occasional disquieting event. The memo for Oct. 9 through 14, 1944, described an "unusual shipment" that arrived at the Kansas City bureau.

"Although marked as consisting of 257 pieces," the memo read, "when opened, the containers were found packed with Graves Registration bags. The total lots of individual effects in the shipment were 8,100, emanating in France."

In 1946, even with the war over, the Effects Bureau still employed about 500 people. They were still processing effects from the war in the Pacific .

2.

Cigar boxes and other containers with the belongings of dead members of the U.S. armed services were processed at Kansas City's Effects Bureau.
Record Group 92

SCENES FROM WAR

Army Signal Corps photographs were given to the Central Plains Region by the Combined Arms Research Library, a military science research center supporting the Army Command and General Staff College at Fort Leavenworth, Kansas.

An Army chaplain baptized soldiers of the 24th Infantry Division in Korea in November 1952, above.
Record Group 338

Two months after the allied landings at Normandy, this Jewish service, left, was conducted in an apple orchard in France. A Star of David mounted on the chaplain's jeep formed the centerpiece.
Record Group 338

2.

By the April 1945, Germany was desperate for troops, as attested to by the faces of these soldiers. Thirteen to 16 years old, they were captured by the U.S. Third Army north of Moosburg, Germany. The prisoners had seen only one month's military service.

Record Group 338

In the 60s, strong feelings

Passions ran high in the Vietnam War era. In Wichita, Kansas, loose talk by one passionate protester got him in trouble with some passionate authorities.

Charles Blackmon, a student at Wichita State University and member of that school's chapter of the Students for a Democratic Society, or SDS, was indicted in November 1967 for threatening the president. That month, President Lyndon Johnson was scheduled to land at nearby McConnell Air Force Base for a brief tour. The SDS chapter met beforehand and evidently, Blackmon grew frustrated at the lack of planning for a protest demonstration.

"I'm going to get a gun and kill the son of a bitch," Blackmon said, according to indictment documents issued the next month.

Among people attending the meeting was an undercover informant. Blackmon was arrested on Nov. 11, shortly before Johnson was scheduled to arrive for his brief Veterans Day tour of the base. Blackmon was charged with threatening "to inflict bodily harm" on the President of the United States, a federal crime. Authorities also tracked down several other members of the same SDS chapter.

To some, the timing was intentional. A Kansas member of the American Civil Liberties Union charged that the actions represented a "high-handed attempt by the military to muzzle criticism of the war in Vietnam."

Blackmon had been active in local anti-war activities. One of the government's exhibits in Blackmon's trial was a photograph of him demonstrating against the war.

The next January the U.S. Secret Service reported that the number of persons arrested each year for threatening the president had quintupled since the assassination of President John F. Kennedy in November 1963. In Kennedy's final year, 80 such arrests were made. In the 12 months ending in June 1967, the number was 425. Following Warren Commission recommendations, over the same period the number of Secret Service agents had increased from 350 to 575.

The Blackmon trial suggests that the agency took such threats seriously.

In May, 1969, a jury found Blackmon not guilty.

Playing the part of a marionette representing South Vietnam, Charles Blackmon took part in this protest against the war in Vietnam.
Record Group 21

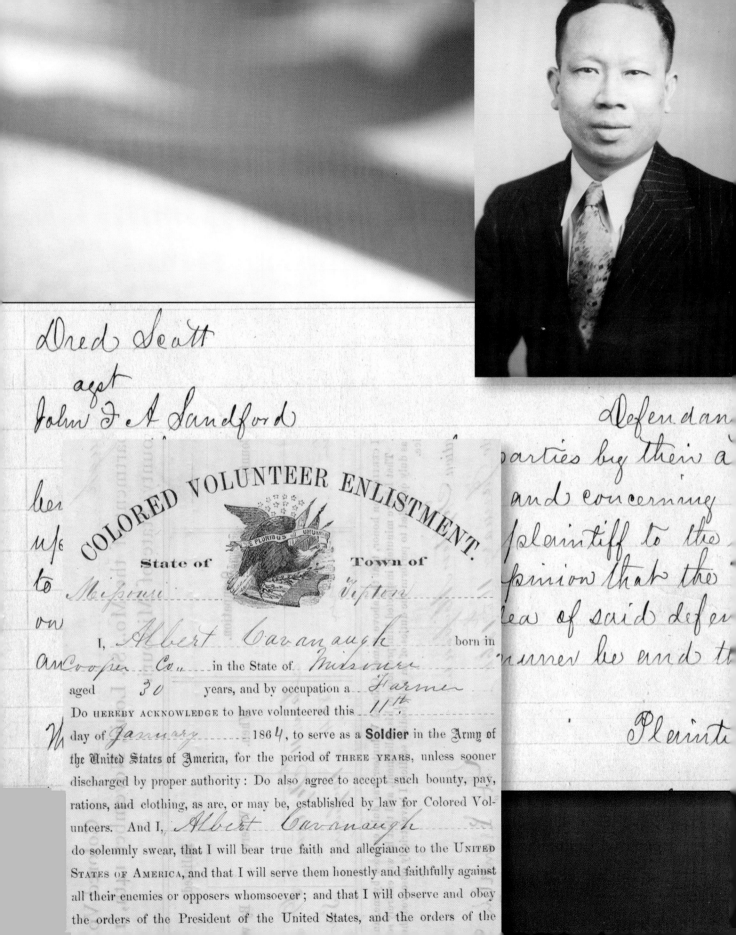

Dred Scott

agst

John F. A. Sandford

Defendan

parties by their a

and concerning

plaintiff to the

pinion that the

ea of said defer

nurrer be and t

Pleinti

COLORED VOLUNTEER ENLISTMENT.

State of _Missouri_   **Town of** _Tipton_

I, _Albert Cavanaugh_ born in _Cooper Co._ in the State of _Missouri_ aged _30_ years, and by occupation a _Farmer_ Do HEREBY ACKNOWLEDGE to have volunteered this _11th_ day of _January_ 1864, to serve as a **Soldier** in the Army of the United States of America, for the period of THREE YEARS, unless sooner discharged by proper authority: Do also agree to accept such bounty, pay, rations, and clothing, as are, or may be, established by law for Colored Volunteers. And I, _Albert Cavanaugh_ do solemnly swear, that I will bear true faith and allegiance to the UNITED STATES OF AMERICA, and that I will serve them honestly and faithfully against all their enemies or opposers whomsoever; and that I will observe and obey the orders of the President of the United States, and the orders of the

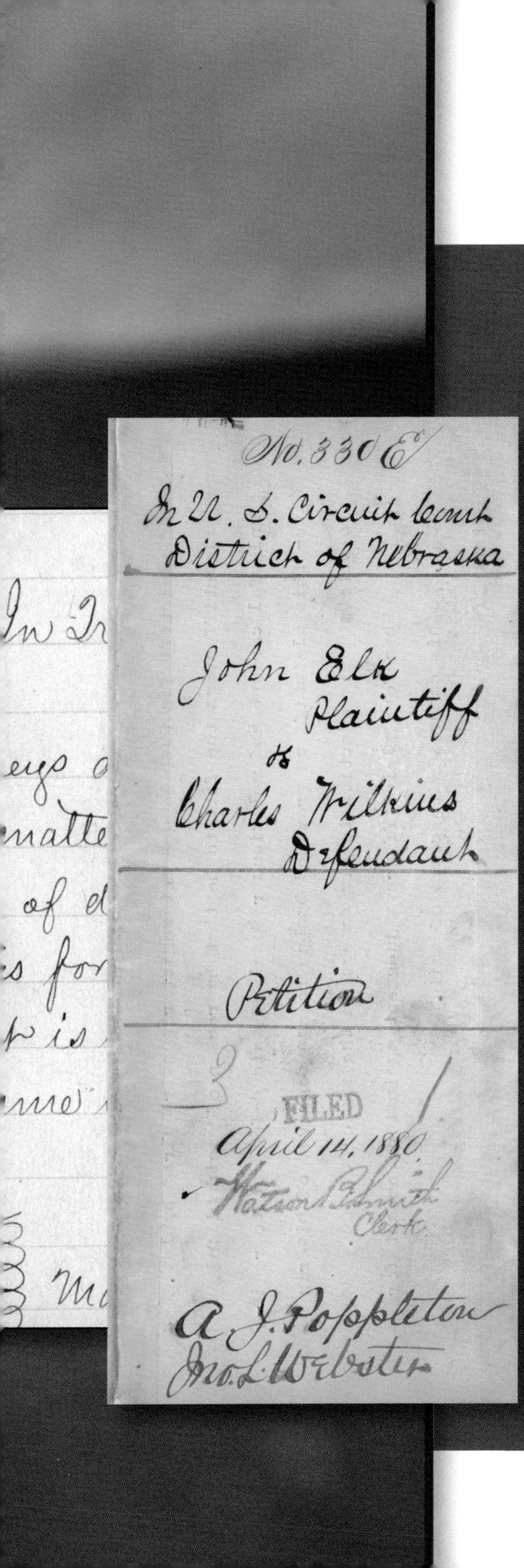

No. 330 E

In U. S. Circuit Court District of Nebraska

John Elk
Plaintiff
vs
Charles Wilkins
Defendant

Petition

FILED
April 14, 1880
Watson B. Smith
Clerk

A. J. Poppleton
Jno. L. Webster

CIVIL RIGHTS— AND WRONGS

In the Civil War, Missouri slave owners loyal to the union could petition the federal government for compensation if their slaves joined the Union Army in the fight against slavery. In World War II, a Japanese name could get you removed to an inland reservation. In the 1950s, black children were assigned to faraway schools if the schools nearest their homes were for whites only.

The first entries in this oversized volume, which served the United States Circuit Court in St. Louis, were dated in 1849. The book contains the court clerk's notes about documents filed in various cases. One of those concerns Dred Scott, the slave who tried and failed to win his freedom in court.

In 1846, Scott sued for his freedom in St. Louis on grounds that his owner had taken him to live in the free state of Illinois and the free territory of Wisconsin before Scott was brought to the slave state of Missouri. The litigation continued over 11 years and eventually reached the U.S. Supreme Court in Washington.

In 1857 Chief Justice Roger Taney ruled that Scott, a black man, could not sue in federal court because he was not a citizen. The decision outraged abolitionists, and fueled their determination to end slavery.

Thus these notes, kept for the U.S. Circuit Court for the District of Missouri, recorded legal skirmishes that led to the Civil War.

John W Martin. Charles Meredeth Samuel H Sone
A. J. Minor for good cause shown be discharged from
on regular panel of petit Jurors at present term of

                    Plaintiff
                                    In Trespass
                    Defendant

ome again the parties by their attorneys and the Court
ntly advised of and concerning the matters of law arising
filed herein by plaintiff to the plea of defendant filed
plaintiff. Is of opinion that the law is for the plaintiff
and that the plea of said defendant is insufficient
the said demurrer be and the same is hereby Sustained

                    Plaintiffs
                                    Manslaughter
Albert W Hardy   Defendants

CLAIM FOR A SOLDIER

In November 1866, Horace Kingsbury of Franklin, Missouri, traveled down the Missouri River to Boonville to file a claim for property that had once belonged to him. That property was Albert Cavanaugh, Kingsbury's former slave, who had enlisted in the U.S. Army.

Two acts of Congress, one in 1864 and the other in 1866, allowed owners of slaves who had enlisted or been drafted into the U.S. military to seek compensation from the federal government — if the owners had been loyal to the Union. Owners could receive up to $300 for slaves who enlisted and up to $100 for slaves who were drafted.

The Emancipation Proclamation freed the slaves in states that rebelled in the Civil War. In border states that remained in the Union, such as Missouri, the compensation was available.

Documents detailed how Kingsbury had purchased Cavanaugh in 1854 from an agent. They also have the signatures of two friends Kingsbury brought to Boonville. They professed that Kingsbury not only had owned Cavanaugh but also been loyal to the United States and not to the "so-called Confederate States of America."

Also documented was Cavanaugh's enlistment in the Colored Volunteers in January 1864 at Tipton, Missouri. In a cursory examination, an Army surgeon noted that Cavanaugh's eyes were brown and that he stood 5 feet 6 inches tall. Evidently unable to write, Cavanaugh made an "x" on the enlistment document next to his name. He identified himself as a farmer, 30 years old. He volunteered for three years, swearing allegiance to the United States.

The government shut down the compensation program in 1867.

This central Missouri slaveowner, Horace Kingsbury, sought compensation for his slave, Albert Cavanaugh, who joined the Union Army in early 1864.
Record Group 21

...on for **Enlisted Slave.**

...bury a *Loyal city* and a resident
County of *Howard* State of
...hereby claim compensation, under the provisions of
...2, Act approved July 28, 1866 for my slave *Albert*
...enlisted *January 11*
...by *Lt. F. Swap*
Regiment, U. S. Colored Troops,
...ment, and a descriptive list, as required, accompanying this

...rnment of the United States, I present the accompanying
...be filed with this application, in accordance with require-
...Adjutant General's Office.

Horace Kingsbur...

...LLEGIANCE.

...the owner and claimant, do solemnly swear that the fore-
...er and owner of the said slave, and that the facts alleged
...t of said slave into the military service of the
...have never joined, *or been concerned in any insurrection or*
...States ; *that I have never given any aid, countenance, counsel*
...whom I had reason to believe were about to engage in
...ited States: *that I have neither sought, nor accepted, nor*
...military, nor to perform any service whatever under any
...ed States : *that I have not yielded a voluntary support to*
...thority, power or constitution within the United States,
...est of my knowledge and ability, I have supported and
...United States *against all enemies, foreign and domestic, and*
...ue *to support, defend and obey, the Constitution and laws of*
...ce to the same ; and that I take this oath freely, without
...me God.

Horace Kingsbur...

...ille mo
...ber 186 6
...son
...ublic

COLORED VOLUNTEER ENLISTMENT.

State of   **Town of**
Missouri   *Tipton*

I, *Albert Cavanaugh* born in
Cooper Co. in the State of *Missouri*
aged *30* years, and by occupation a *Farmer*
Do HEREBY ACKNOWLEDGE to have volunteered this *11th*
day of *January* 186 *4*, to serve as a **Soldier** in the Army of
the United States of America, for the period of THREE YEARS, unless sooner
discharged by proper authority : Do also agree to accept such bounty, pay,
rations, and clothing, as are, or may be, established by law for Colored Volunteers. And I, *Albert Cavanaugh*
do solemnly swear, that I will bear true faith and allegiance to the UNITED
STATES OF AMERICA, and that I will serve them honestly and faithfully against
all their enemies or opposers whomsoever ; and that I will observe and obey
the orders of the President of the United States, and the orders of the
officers appointed over me, according to the Rules and Articles of War.

BORN HERE, CAN'T VOTE

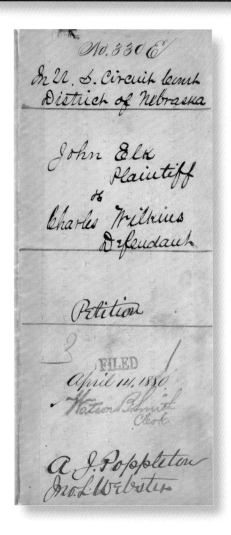

In April 1880 John Elk tried to register to vote in Omaha, Nebraska. Charles Wilkins, an election official in Omaha's fifth ward, turned him down. Elk was an Indian.

Because he had been born in the United States, Elk believed he was a citizen by virtue of the 14th Amendment. In addition, under the provisions of the 15th Amendment, he believed he should not be prevented from registering to vote on the basis of his race or color.

In a court petition he filed in 1880, Elk said that he had severed his relations with the Winnebago tribe and surrendered himself to the jurisdiction of the United States.

He lost his first case in federal circuit court. He appealed to the U.S. Supreme Court, but in 1884 it upheld the decision of the lower court. The Supreme Court ruled that the 14th Amendment did not bestow citizenship on Indians and that the 15th Amendment didn't apply to him.

In 1890 the Indian Naturalization Act granted citizenship to American Indians if they applied for it. In 1924 the Indian Citizenship Act granted citizenship to all American Indians born in the United States.

John Elk made his mark, an "X," on his plea over being refused the chance to vote.
Record Group 21

requested the right to vote where said Wilkins who was then acting as one of the Judges of said election in said ward in further carrying out his wilful and malicious designs aforesaid declared to plaintiff and to the other election officers that plaintiff was an Indian and not a citizen and not entitled to vote, and said Judges and Clerk's of election refused to receive the vote of plaintiff for that he was not registered as required by law.

Plaintiff avers the fact to be that by reason of said wilful unlawful corrupt and malicious refusal of said defendant to register this plaintiff as provided by Law he was deprived of his right to vote at said election to his damage in the sum of $6,000.

Wherefore plaintiff prays judgment against defendant for $6,000 his damages with costs of suit.

State of Nebraska

Douglas County   SS

A. J. Poppleton
Jno L. Webster
     Atty's for Plaintiff

John Elk being first duly sworn deposes and says that he has heard read the contents of the foregoing Petition and that the facts therein stated are true as he verily believes.

      his
John x *ELK*
     mark

Sworn to before me and subscribed in my presence this 14th day of April 1880.

Edward W. Simeral
     Notary Public
   in and for Douglas
     County State of Nebraska

PROVING BIRTH

In 1933 Lee Kim was arrested in Chicago on a narcotics charge. He was convicted and sentenced to one year and a day in the U.S. penitentiary at Leavenworth, Kansas.

Federal immigration officials noted Kim's imprisonment and sought to prove that he was not an American citizen. That way, Kim could be deported. But if Kim could convince the court of his citizenship he could stay in the United States.

Because he was imprisoned in Kansas, the *United States v. Lee Kim* was heard by the U.S. District Court in Topeka.

From the late 19th century through the 1940s, various arms of the federal government had sought to curtail immigration from China. Chinese exclusion laws were in place by the 1880s. One apparent concern driving these measures was the large number of Chinese who had come to the United States to fulfill the need for inexpensive labor.

During interviews with immigration officials Kim swore that he had been born in San Francisco in 1895. But he couldn't produce a birth certificate or any kind of written documentation of his own life. He claimed his parents had been killed shortly after the 1906 San Francisco earthquake when he was a child.

A cousin, he said, had brought him to Chicago, where he had lived since.

In 1935 a federal judge chose to believe Kim, and ruled that he indeed had been born in San Francisco in 1895 and that he should be released from immigration authorities.

Chinese exclusion policies were repealed in the 1940s. By then, federal authorities were focusing on the threat they believed was represented by another Asian ethnic group — Japanese Americans.

IN T

Unit

Lee

His parents and all records of his birth were destroyed in the San Francisco earthquake and fire, Lee Kim contended.
Record Group 21

3

RICT COURT OF THE UNITED STATES FOR THE DISTRICT OF
    KANSAS, FIRST DIVISION

es of America,   Complainant,

    vs.   No. 3889, Law.

as Lee K:

      My correct name is Lee Kim. I sometimes use the
name Lee Kim Kang. I was born in San Francisco California
on Depont Street May 3rd, 1895. I am an American citizen.
I have no birth certificate or documentary evidence to show
I am an American citizen. My father was born in China and
his name was Lee Chee. He died in 1906 at the time of the
earthquake. My mother's name was Ng Shee. She was born in
China and was killed with my father. I attended chinese
school at San Francisco. Two days before theearthquake, my
mother sent me to assist my cousin, Lee Yuen Que in his drug
store while he was sick. The drug stock was on Dupont Street.
I lived with my cousin after the earthquake who was proprietor
of the Bow Tuse Tong drug store and worked there for some two
or three months. Afterwards I was taken to Chicago by a
cousin, Lee King Yong.

BATTLING DISCRIMINATION

Eventually a justice of the U.S. Supreme Court, Thurgood Marshall battled for decades to end racial discrimination, and some of his most important campaigns took place on the Great Plains.

It was *Brown v. Board of Education of Topeka* that Marshall, as NAACP counsel, appealed to the U.S. Supreme Court in the early 1950s. But Marshall pursued similar cases as well.

Marshall joined the NAACP legal staff in 1936. Nine years later he represented a black elementary school teacher in Festus, a town about 35 miles south of downtown St. Louis.

In *Emma Jane Lee v. Board of Education of Festus* — a class-action suit on behalf of Lee and her black colleagues — Marshall argued that white teachers and principals with basically the same training, qualifications and experience as Lee earned more than she did. That, he said, violated the 14th Amendment.

Indeed, Lee was qualified. She had a college degree and had taken courses at Columbia University in New York. She was in her sixth year of teaching in the Festus district. Nevertheless, she earned less than white teachers with equal or less experience. According to a chart included in the case, several white teachers in the Festus district earned $1,035 a year while Lee earned $765.

Justice wasn't long in arriving. The complaint was filed in June, and a judgment rendered by August. The Festus Board of Education resolved that it would make the pay scale equal.

In January 1952, Marshall returned to Missouri, appearing in Kansas City federal court on behalf of three black Kansas Citians who were turned away from the Swope Park Pool because they were black. The first plaintiff listed in *Williams v. Kansas City* was Esther Williams — not the movie star but a dietician at Kansas City General Hospital No. 2, the public hospital for black patients.

Marshall argued that the rights of the three patrons under the equal protection clause of the 14th Amendment had been violated. He insisted that the separate pool that Kansas City black residents were allowed to visit, built in 1939 for $60,000, was not equal to the Swope Park pool, built in 1942 for $534,000. A federal judge agreed and the city appealed. The Swope Park pool was closed for two summers before an appeals court affirmed the ruling and the U.S. Supreme Court declined to review it.

The swimming pool lawsuit was one of many brought by the NAACP in the 1950s as it whittled away at the nation's segregation laws.

In view of the resolution
Education of Festus, Missouri, set ou
there is no occasion to grant further
The taxable court costs to

CONSENTED TO BY:

Thurgood Marshall
Attorneys for Plaintiff

Thompson, Mitchell, Thompson & Young
and R. Fowler Buckley
Attorneys for Defendants

On May 17 a conference was held between defendants' attorney and plaintiff's attorneys, the said David M. Grant of St. Louis, Missouri and Thurgood Marshall of New York City. Defendants' attorney then conferred with defendants and on May 21 communicated with Mr. Grant and inquired of him as to what, in his opinion, were the positions held by white teachers in Festus comparable to those occupied by the colored teachers; and consequently what salaries he thought his clients were entitled to.

Mr. Grant contended that the following were comparable teachers:

Negro High School NAME	SALARY	Alleged Comparable White Teacher NAME	SALARY
A. C. Shropshire	$1,330.	Ralph B. Tynes	$1,615.
Helen Jones	720.	Magdalene Berger	1,215.
William Willis	855.	Leonard Bryant	1,350.

Negro Elementary School NAME	SALARY	Alleged Comparable White Teacher NAME	SALARY
Fannie Ellis	$ 765.	Katherine England	$ 945.
Elizabeth Engrum	720.	Ruth Juncker	900.
Emma Jane Lee	765.	Dorothy Rohr	1,035.

The amounts demanded by Mr. Grant would require an increase in the total annual salaries to be paid to the negro teachers of $1,905. above the amounts paid for the year 1942-43; or an increase of $1,585. above the amounts already contracted for, for the year 1943-44. Defendants' counsel informed Mr. Grant that it would be necessary for the School _ _ d to meet and give consideration to the problem.

Thereafter the School Board of Festus met and pursuant to _ _ authorization, on June 1, 1943, defendants' counsel wrote David _ rant the letter which is set forth in full in paragraph XXII of _ answer.

ndant Board of
is deemed that
the plaintiff.
the defendants.

idge

Legal documents in the case of *Emma Jane Lee vs. the Board of Education of Festus, Missouri.*
Record Group 21

UNDER SUSPICION

In February 1942, barely two months after Japanese warplanes attacked Pearl Harbor, President Franklin Roosevelt signed Executive Order 9066. It forced more than 100,000 Americans of Japanese descent into internment camps, often called "relocation centers." Based on fears that they could provide aid to an enemy, the order removed Japanese Americans living in a 50-mile-wide area along the Pacific coast from Washington through California, and into southern Arizona.

They were transferred inland; this map details one such internment camp in Colorado.

The order was challenged in court but the U.S. Supreme Court upheld the policy, saying the perceived threat to the country justified the practice.

The last camp closed by the end of 1945.

In 1988 President Ronald Reagan signed the Civil Liberties Act of 1988, approved by Congress to provide an apology for the action, as well as payments of $20,000 to surviving internees.

Plan for an internment camp near Granada on the plains of southeastern Colorado. The camp opened in August 1942 and closed in October 1945. It housed as many as 7,300 people.
Record Group 103

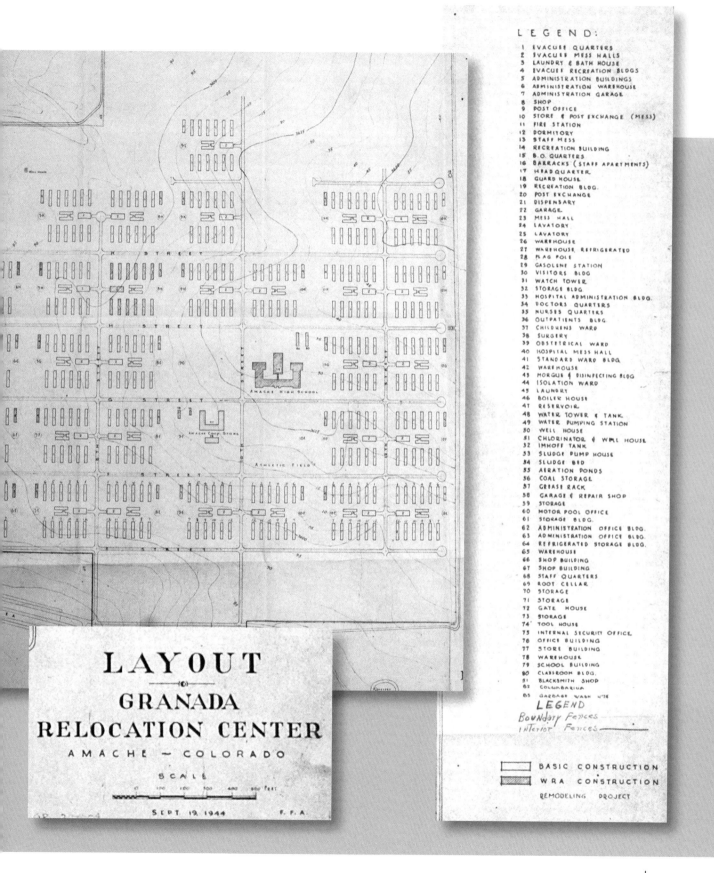

GETTING INTO SCHOOL — OR NOT

In January 1939 Lucile Bluford, a 27-year-old Kansas City journalist, traveled to Columbia, Missouri, to enroll for graduate school work at the University of Missouri School of Journalism.

She had submitted her credentials by mail, among them her bachelor's degree in journalism from the University of Kansas. When she arrived to register at Missouri, Registrar S.W. Canada turned her down.

Bluford was black, and the University of Missouri was segregated.

She tried again in August. Again, Canada denied her a permit to enroll.

As managing editor of the *The Call*, an African-American weekly newspaper in Kansas City, Bluford had followed the efforts of Charles Houston, special counsel for the National Association for the Advancement of Colored People, or NAACP. In 1935 Houston had resolved to target segregation in public education.

One of his first battles was on behalf of Lloyd Gaines, an African-American who had sought entry into the University of Missouri law school.

When Gaines lost his case in Missouri, Houston appealed the ruling to the U.S. Supreme Court. In 1938 the high court ruled in favor of Gaines. Gaines, however, disappeared in a mystery still unresolved. Because he couldn't be found, the case was dismissed.

About that time, Bluford wrote Houston. Soon, working with a legal team headed by Houston and lawyers from St. Louis and Kansas City, Bluford made her first attempt to enroll. After Missouri rebuffed her, Houston sued the university on Bluford's behalf. Bluford ultimately lost, but the litigation prompted establishment of a journalism program at Lincoln University in Jefferson City.

Meanwhile, Bluford continued her journalism career at the *The Call*, detailing the emerging civil rights movement both in Kansas City and across the country. She reported on the campaign in 1958 and 1959 to integrate the dining rooms of downtown Kansas City department stores, as well as the city's successful public accommodations referendum in 1964.

In 1984, the University of Missouri awarded Bluford a Missouri Honor Medal for Distinguished Service in Journalism. The university added an honorary doctorate in 1989, fifty years after she had tried to enroll there.

When Bluford died in 2003 at age 91, former Kansas City Mayor Emanuel Cleaver said "She fought bigotry in her personal life, and then she forced Missouri to face it."

IN THE UNITED STATES DISTRICT COURT FOR THE CENTRAL DIVISION

OF THE WESTERN DISTRICT OF MISSOURI

Lucile Bluford,

           Plaintiff,

    vs.   Civil Action
                         No. 42

S. W. Canada,

           Defendant.

BRIEF IN SUPPORT OF DEFENDANT'S
MOTION TO DISMISS

      This is a damage suit, in two counts. The plaintiff
alleges that on January 30, 1939, and again on September 14,
1939, the defendant registrar of the University of Missouri
refused to issue to plaintiff, a negro citizen of Missouri, a
permit to register as a student in the University of Missouri
for graduate work in journalism. (Plaintiff alleges that she
is a graduate of the University of Kansas with the degree of
Bachelor of Arts with major in journalism.) For each of the
alleged refusals to issue the permit, plaintiff asks $10,000.00
damages, a total of $20,000.00 in the two counts.

      The complaint alleges that defendant's refusals to
issue permits violated the Equal Protection Clause of the
Fourteenth Amendment and Section 41 of Title 8, U.S.Code, and
rendered defendant liable under Section 43 of Title 8, U. S.
Code. The latter section provides:

      "Every person who, under color of any statute,
ordinance, regulation, custom, or usage, of any state
or territory, subjects, or causes to be subjected,

Missouri's defense of its actions turning down the application of Lucile Bluford.
Record Group 21

Defendant's motion to dismiss is based upon the ground that each count of the complaint fails to state a claim upon which relief can be granted. It is submitted that the motion should be sustained, for the following reasons:

I

The laws and long established public policy of the State of Missouri provide for and require separation of the white and negro races for purposes of higher education; and such provision is valid.

That the laws and public policy of the state provide for and require race separation in higher education was expressly ruled in the first opinion in the Gaines Case (State ex rel. Gaines v. Canada, 113 S.W. (2d) 783,787.) The holding on that point was followed by the Supreme Court of the United States in State of Missouri vs. Canada, 59 Sup. Ct. Rep. 232, 234, where the court, after reviewing the holding on that point, said:

"In that view it necessarily followed that the curators of the University of Missouri acted in accordance with the policy of the state in denying petitioner admission to its School of Law upon the sole ground of his race."

A provision for race separation for the purposes of education is valid. In the Gaines Case the Supreme Court of the United States recognized this to be true. In referring to the obligation of the state to provide negroes with advantages for higher education substantially equal to the advantages afforded to white students, the court said (59 Sup. Ct. Rep. 232, 234):

IN THE DISTRICT COURT OF THE UNITED STATES FOR THE CENTRAL DIVISION
OF THE WESTERN DISTRICT OF MISSOURI

Lucile Bluford,   Plaintiff,

       vs.   No. 128

S. W. Canada,   Defendant.

VERDICT

We, the jury in the above entitled cause, find the issues
herein in favor of the defendant and against the plaintiff.

Charles E. Abbott
Foreman

A LONG WAY TO A SEGREGATED SCHOOL

To reach the all-black school to which she was assigned, third-grader Linda Brown had to travel a mile through a railroad switchyard in Topeka, Kansas. An elementary school for white students was closer.

So testified Oliver Brown, a minister and railroad welder, in the case of *Brown v. Board of Education of Topeka*.

It was the early 1950s and Topeka schools, like public schools in many other parts of the country, were segregated. The Topeka branch of the National Association for the Advancement of Colored People, believing school segregation had grown intolerable, spoke with several black parents about participating in litigation. Brown agreed to testify.

The NAACP went to court, requesting an injunction against the Topeka Board of Education, and a federal court heard the case in June 1951.

A three-judge panel found no "substantial discrimination" in the operation of schools. The judges relied on *Plessy v. Ferguson*, the 1896 Supreme Court decision that advanced the "separate but equal" doctrine allowing segregation if equal facilities were offered to blacks and whites. In a supplement to their decision, though, the judges echoed the testimony of educators who had argued that the segregation of students in public schools had a "detrimental effect" upon black children.

The NAACP appealed the ruling in October 1951. Eventually, the case was consolidated with lawsuits challenging school segregation in South Carolina, Virginia, Delaware and the District of Columbia.

On May 17, 1954, the U.S. Supreme Court ruled unanimously that "separate educational facilities are inherently unequal." Linda Brown's case was listed first and so one of the most important rulings in American history bore her name.

Oliver Brown died in 1961.

"I think it is sad that he could not live long enough to know that anytime equal rights are being championed, *Brown v. Board* is always used as the basis," Cheryl Brown Henderson, a daughter of Oliver Brown and sister to Linda Henderson, told *The Kansas City Star* in 2004, on the 50th anniversary of the ruling.

"I think that is pretty profound."

Oliver Brown describes the distance his daughter must go to get to her segregated school.
Record Group 21

A.   511 West First Street.

Q.   Are you a citizen of the United States?

A.   I am.

Q.   And you are a plaintiff in this lawsuit.

A.   I am.

                    JUDGE HUXMAN: Talk a little louder, Mr.
Brown.

                    JUDGE MELLOTT: He didn't answer yet.

                    THE WITNESS: Yes.

Q.   (By Mr. Bledsoe) What is your business or occupation?

A.   Carman welder.

                    MR. BLEDSOE: Speak a little louder.

                    THE WITNESS: A carman welder.

                    JUDGE HUXMAN: Mr. Brown, it's difficult
to hear you. I wish you would make an effort to speak
so we can hear you distinctly; we want to hear what you
say.

Q.   (By Mr. Bledsoe) Are you married?

A.   Yes.

Q.   And, if so, who constitutes the members of your family?

A.   I do.

Q.   What I mean by that, who constitute the members of your
family?

A.   I have a wife and three children.

Q.   What are the ages of your children?

A. My oldest daughter is eight years old; I have one four and another one five months.

Q. What is the name of your daughter, oldest daughter?

A. Linda Carol Brown.

Q. In what school district or territory do you live, Mr. Brown?

A. I live in the Sumner District.

Q. Sumner School District.

A. Yes.

MR. BLEDSOE: For the purpose of the record if the Court please, let it be shown that the witness resides in Sumner School District. I think it's this district here marked (indicating on exhibit) -- that is colored red.

JUDGE MELLOTT: Well, I am afraid your testimony standing alone isn't too intelligent; it isn't to me. Now, as I understand it, Topeka is one school district, you agreed at the pre-trial, but you said that there were certain territories.

MR. BLEDSOE: Well, I may substitute territory for -- if I may -- territory for district.

JUDGE HUXMAN: Wouldn't it be more helpful to the Court if you just had these witnesses locate their residence with reference to the colored school that they attend, rather than having it defined by the various ter-

ritories. That is the important factor, how far they are
from school.

Q. (By Mr. Bledsoe) Now, Mr. Brown, where do you live with
reference to Monroe School?

A. Well, stated that I live at 511 West First Street which is
fifteen blocks, approximately, from Monroe School.

        MR. GOODELL: I didn't get that.

        JUDGE MELLOTT: Fifteen blocks from Monroe
School.

        THE WITNESS: Twenty-one blocks, pardon me;
approximately twenty-one blocks.

Q. (By Mr. Bledsoe) You are talking about now the way your
daughter has to travel to go to Monroe School, is that
correct?

A. That is true.

Q. Does your daughter ride the school bus?

A. Yes.

Q. All right. Now, Mr. Brown, what time does your daughter
leave home in the morning to walk to First and Quincy,
the bus pick-up point, to go to school; what time does
she leave home?

A. She leaves at twenty minutes 'till eight o'clock.

Q. Twenty minutes of eight.

A. Every school morning.

Q. What time, or thereabouts, does she board the bus at

First and Quincy?

A. Well, she is supposed to be there at eight o'clock and which she has been, in many instances, but many times she has had to wait through the cold, the rain and the snow until the bus got there, not knowing definitely what time it gets there all the time.

Q. All right. Now, Mr. Brown, she boards that bus about eight o'clock. What time does she arrive at the school?

A. She's supposed to arrive at the school around 8:30.

Q. Eight thirty. And, as I understand it, what time does the classes begin at school?

A. Nine o'clock.

Q. What does your daughter do between the time the bus arrives at the school at 8:30 and 9:00 o'clock?

A. Well, there is sometimes she has had to wait outside the school until someone came to let them in, through the winter season and likewise, many times.

Q. What else does she do, if anything?

A. Well, there is nothing she can do except stand out and clap her hands to keep them warm or jump up and down. They have no provisions at all to shelter them.

Q. And what you want the Court to understand is that your daughter is conveyed to the school, she gets there by 8:30 in the morning, and that she has nothing to do until school starts at 9:00 o'clock, is that right?

A.   That is correct.

Q.   Now, Mr. Brown, you don't -- withdraw that, please. What provisions are made by the school board for your daughter to have warm lunch, if any.

A.   There are no provisions made at all.

        JUDGE HUXMAN: Mr. Bledsoe, hasn't it been agreed and testified to by Dr. McFarland that no provision is made for warm lunches?

        MR. BLEDSOE: I beg your pardon; I believe you are correct, if the Court please.

        JUDGE HUXMAN: That stands admitted, doesn't it?

        MR. BLEDSOE: That's right; that is all right. Let me withdraw that, please.

Q.   (By Mr. Bledsoe) Now, then, your child -- you don't get to see your child during the daytime until she returns home in the evening, is that right?

A.   That is correct, sir.

Q.   Would you, Mr. Brown, would you like to have your daughter home, have the same opportunity of giving her parental guidance as the white fathers and mothers might do their child.

A.   Yes, sir.

        MR. GOODELL: We object to the form of that question as assuming a state of facts not in evidence and, in fact, contrary to some of the admitted stipulation of facts.

> JUDGE HUXMAN: The objection will be sustained.

Q. (By Mr. Bledsoe) But you do not see your daughter from the time she leaves in the morning until she returns in the evening, is that correct?

A. I do not.

Q. What time is that?

A. She gets home around fifteen minutes to five.

Q. Fifteen minutes to five. Do you know whether or not there is any provisions made to shelter or protect your daughter while she is standing on the street or the designated bus pick-up --

> JUDGE HUXMAN: Mr. Bledsoe, that has been testified to, and I think it's conceded no shelter is provided in any of these points where colored children are picked up, is that not so, Mr. Goodell?

> MR. GOODELL: That's right.

Q. (By Mr. Bledsoe) Now, Mr. Brown, what is the condition of the area there between your residence and First and Quincy where your daughter boards the bus?

A. Well, there are a considerable amount of railroad tracks there; they do a vast amount of switching from the Rock Island yards and from the time that she leaves home until

she gets to Quincy, First and Quincy, to board the bus,
she has to pass all of these switch tracks and she --
also including the main thoroughfare, Kansas Avenue and
First; there is a vast amount of traffic there morning
and evening when she goes and returns. There is no provisions at all made for safety precautions to protect
those children passing these thoroughfares at all.

Q. Now, Mr. Brown, if your daughter were permitted to attend Sumner School would there be any such obstructions
or any such conditions as she will meet on her way to
First and Quincy?

A. Not hardly as I know of.

Q. How far is it from your residence to Sumner School?

A. Seven blocks.

Q. Seven blocks. Mr. Brown, are you assessed a tax for the
support and maintenance of the public schools of the City
of Topeka?

A. I am.

      MR. GOODELL: We object to that, if the
Court please; it's wholly outside the scope --

      JUDGE HUXMAN: He may answer.

      THE WITNESS: I am, sir.

Q. (By Mr. Bledsoe) Mr. Brown, do you consider it an advantage to have a school in the neighborhood in which you
live near your home? Do you consider that an advantage?

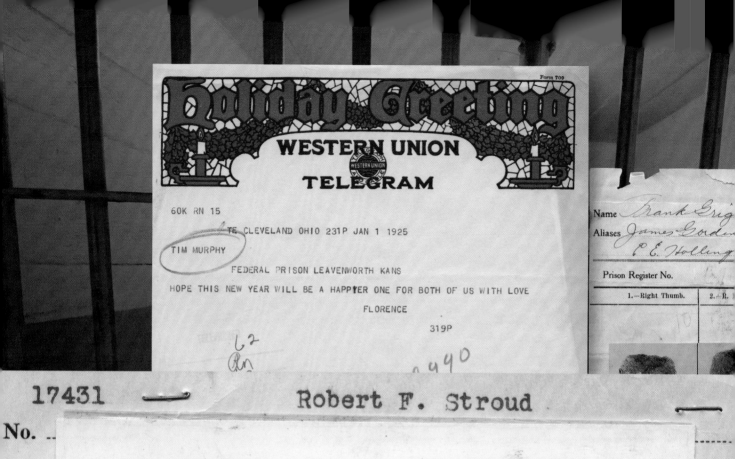

Form 709

Holiday Greeting

WESTERN UNION
TELEGRAM

60K RN 15

TE CLEVELAND OHIO 231P JAN 1 1925

TIM MURPHY

FEDERAL PRISON LEAVENWORTH KANS

HOPE THIS NEW YEAR WILL BE A HAPPIER ONE FOR BOTH OF US WITH LOVE

FLORENCE

319P

Name *Frank Grig*
Aliases *James Gordon*
          C. E. Holling

Prison Register No.

1.—Right Thumb.   2.—R.

17431

Robert F. Stroud

No.

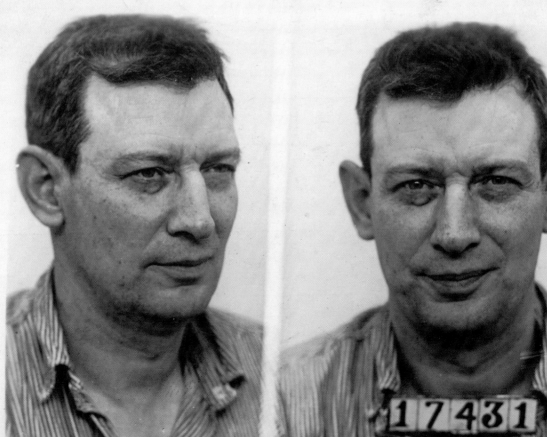

17431

M IS NOT TO BE PINNED

MALE

Classification No.

7351 10   25 W I0 14

GHT HAND.   9 U 00 17

3.—R. Middle Finger.	4.—R. Third Finger.	5.—R. Little Finger.

FT HAND.

8.—L. Middle Finger.	9.—L. Third Finger.	10.—L. Little Finger.

DOING TIME

Getting in trouble with the man has consequences. The U.S. Penitentiary in Leavenworth, Kansas, is one of them. Step over the line and you might wind up there. Indeed, "Leavenworth" long ago entered the language as shorthand for prison. The Central Plains Region holds 68,937 Leavenworth inmate case files, according to a recent tally. Some files contain familiar names, such as Robert Stroud, the "Birdman of Alcatraz," who did much of his research on birds at Leavenworth before being transferred to the California prison in 1942. There's a file on Jack Johnson, the first African-American heavyweight boxing champion, who spent several months in residence in Leavenworth in the early 1920s. More often the Leavenworth files contain less-familiar names, and document the grim reality of obscure lives under close observation. The files even serve genealogists who want to learn about family members whose names weren't always mentioned at the dinner table. Not every federal lawbreaker on the Great Plains wound up in Leavenworth. For Carl Austin Hall and Bonnie Heady, who kidnapped and murdered a 6-year-old boy in 1953, justice was swift. Captured in October, they were sentenced to death in November and executed before the year was out.

THE BIRDMAN OF LEAVENWORTH

Burt Lancaster was no Robert Stroud — and he could thank his lucky stars. Stroud gained worldwide fame as the "Birdman of Alcatraz" after Lancaster portrayed him in the 1962 film of that name. The movie showed Stroud, serving a life sentence for murder, pursuing painstaking research on birds. Stroud's work led to two books.

To bird lovers, at least, and to fans of the movie, Stroud appeared to have some redeeming social value. Some of those who encountered Stroud found him repellent.

James J. Fisher, a longtime reporter for *The Kansas City Times* and *Star*, once wrote of seeing Stroud in a holding cell at the federal penitentiary in Leavenworth in the early 1960s.

The prisoner, awaiting an appearance in Kansas City federal court, passed the time by yelling lewd suggestions through the bars, Fisher recalled.

Stroud spent 54 years in federal prisons, many of those years in solitary confinement. Although the title of the movie referred to the federal penitentiary in San Francisco Bay, Stroud conducted most of his avian research at Leavenworth.

A Leavenworth reference card, apparently completed in the early 1940s, lists Stroud's IQ at 116, a nudge above normal. Under the category of avocational interests, prison officials noted, "Scientific Study of Birds."

Stroud claimed no religious denomination. To describe his mental condition, officials simply wrote "Negative."

Other documents tell how Leavenworth officials allowed him to ship birds nationwide (in November 1942 he charged $10 for a canary shipped to a woman in Minneapolis) and how he was transferred to Alcatraz in December 1942.

Stroud was only 19 when he first went to federal prison in 1909 for killing a bartender in Alaska. He didn't prove a model prisoner. After guards learned that he was attempting to traffic in narcotics behind bars, officials transferred him to the U.S. Penitentiary in Leavenworth. There, Stroud killed a prison guard with a knife in a crowded mess hall and eventually was sentenced to hang. After Stroud's mother pleaded for his life, President Woodrow Wilson reduced the sentence to life.

In 1920, during a 30-minute exercise period, Stroud came upon a nest of tiny sparrows on the prison grounds. He took the helpless birds back to his cell, and found his calling. Over time prison guards granted his requests for books and equipment for his research.

Stroud died in his sleep at age 73 at the U.S. Medical Center for Federal Prisoners in Springfield, Missouri. He had been there since 1959.

Fisher, in a column years later, noted that Stroud had been an early media darling, drawing some of his first attention from the Kansas City papers in the 1930s. But upon Stroud's death, the nation's press was distracted. His body was discovered on Nov. 21, 1963, at the Springfield federal facility. His death was announced the next day when, as Fisher wrote, "there was other news" — the assassination of President John F. Kennedy.

FPI Inc—LK—11-20-40—15M— 6-1

UNITED STATES
PENAL AND CORRECTIONAL INSTITUTIONS

Leavenworth, Kansas.
(Institution)

November 12, 1942. , 19

Authorization to Mail Packages out of Institution

Robert Stroud, , Register No. # 17431
(Name of Inmate)

s authorized to ship from the institution the following items to the address given below:

(One Bird, Value $ 10.00

Express Collect
Valuation, $ 10.00

Arrangements have been made for collection of commissary coupo
ove named inmate, to cover cost of this shipment.

The articles indicated above were packed in my presence in accordanc

To   Bertha M. Hayden.
(Name)

4937 Colfax Ave.
(Box No. or Street Address)

(of address
shown on
label)

26	27	28	29	30	31	32	33	34	35	36	37	38	39	40	41	42	43	44	45	46	47	48	49	50

SHOES ISSUED

REGISTER NO. 17431   NAME Robt F Stroud

REC'D.   EXPIRATION Life   SIZE

DATE	WORK	CANVAS	DISCHARGE	SPECIAL	REPAIRED	REMARKS
MAR 18 1938	2					
OCT 28 1938	2					
JAN 29 1940	197		returned Austom 1-30-40			
MAR 6 1940	#6					
FEB 17 1941	6					
JUN 11 1942	6					

DISCHARGED DEC 10 1942

TRANSFERRED TO ALCATRAZ

FPI Inc—FLK—2-6-37—1000—6110-37

(City)

JAG 300
Rev. Oct. 1940

ASSOCIATE WARDEN'S RECORD CARD

Offense Murder
Sentence Life   Begins 2-28-1922
Date Imp 5-10-1920   At D Kansas
Date Rec'd 2-28-1922
Par. Elig 2-27-1937
C. R. Life   Max Life
Comm. Fine   G. T.

PREVIOUS RECORD:
Jails   Ref.
Pens: Fed. 1   State
Detainers: Fed.   State
Escapes: Fed.   State
CUSTODY: Maximum
Crimes Involved: (Enumerate)

    1 Previous term for Murder

Aliases:

Race White   Age 1890
Married Single   Deps 0
Citizen Yes   Relig None
Physical Cond. Light Duty
Mental Cond. Negative
Education: S.A.T.
          G.S.CE - College Level
PSYCHOLOGICAL and APTITUDE TEST:
MA 18-6
IQ 116
Occupational Skills:

Avocational Interests:
Scientific Study of Birds

History of Occupational Experience

Occupations	No. Yrs.	Verification of Performance	
		Quality	Dependability
None			

17431

Name	Number	Residence	Occupations		
STROUD, Robert	17431-L	Unknown	None		5

Among Robert Stroud's records was one for the sale and delivery of a bird to a buyer in Minnesota.
Record Group 129

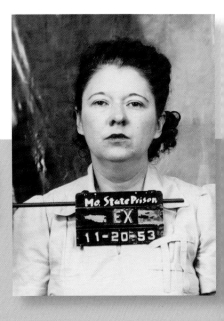

COLD-BLOODED KILLERS

Perhaps their faces give a clue to their deed, and perhaps not. They are Carl Austin Hall and Bonnie Heady, who in 1953 kidnapped and killed 6-year-old Bobby Greenlease.

On September 28 Heady took Bobby from his private Kansas City school on a ruse, identifying herself as an aunt of the child and saying that Bobby's mother had suffered a heart attack.

Afterward, Hall and Heady contacted Bobby's parents, wealthy Kansas City Cadillac dealer Robert Greenlease and his wife, Virginia. They told the Greenleases that the child was safe, and they demanded ransom for his return.

In fact, Hall and Heady had taken Bobby to farmland in Johnson County, Kansas, where they shot and killed him. They drove his body to St. Joseph, Missouri, and buried it behind Heady's house.

Knowing none of this, the Greenlease family arranged to pay Hall and Heady $600,000 ransom in cash. Arthur Eisenhower, brother of President Dwight Eisenhower and a Kansas City bank official, helped the Greenlease family assemble the ransom in $10 and $20 bills.

St. Louis police arrested Hall and Heady in October.

Under the Lindbergh Act, passed after the 1932 kidnapping and killing of the toddler son of aviator Charles Lindbergh, the interstate transport of a kidnapping victim was a federal crime.

The two pleaded guilty and on November 19, 1953, after deliberating for an hour, a jury in Kansas City federal court recommended the death penalty for both Hall and Heady. They died December 18 in the Missouri State Penitentiary gas chamber.

"Assuredly, a more heinous crime cannot be conceived," FBI Director J. Edgar Hoover wrote in a wire service article that directed parents, schools and youth organizations to review school checkout procedures.

Hall and Heady, their indictment and the jury's recommended punishment: execution.
Record Groups 118(photos) and 21(court documents)

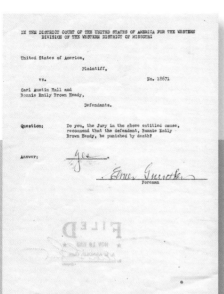

IN THE DISTRICT COURT OF THE UNITED STATES OF AMERICA FOR THE WESTERN
DIVISION OF THE WESTERN DISTRICT OF MISSOURI

United States of America,

        Plaintiff,

    vs.   No. 18671

Carl Austin Hall and
Bonnie Emily Brown Heady,

        Defendants.

Question: Do you, the Jury in the above entitled cause,
            recommend that the defendant, Bonnie Emily
            Brown Heady, be punished by death?

Answer: yes.

              Ernes Guenther
                   Foreman

FILED

IN THE DISTRICT COURT OF THE UNITED STATES OF AMERICA FOR THE WESTERN
DIVISION OF THE WESTERN DISTRICT OF MISSOURI

United States of America,

        Plaintiff,

    vs.   No. 18671

Carl Austin Hall and
Bonnie Emily Brown Heady,

        Defendants.

Question: Do you, the Jury in the above entitled cause,
            recommend that the defendant, Carl Austin Hall,
            be punished by death?

Answer: yes.

              Ernes Guenther
                   Foreman

FILED

United States of America,   )   **#18671**

          Plaintiff,)

)   Section 1201, Title 18,

    vs.   )   United States Code

Carl Austin Hall   )

   and   )

Bonnie Emily Brown Heady,)

)

          Defendants.)

I-N-D-I-C-T-M-E-N-T

The Grand Jury Charges:

    That on or about the 28th day of September, 1953, the
above named defendants, Carl Austin Hall and Bonnie Emily Brown
Heady, did unlawfully, knowingly, wilfully and feloniously trans-
port in interstate commerce from Kansas City, Jackson County,
Missouri, in the Western Division of the Western District of
Missouri, into the State of Kansas one Robert Cosgrove Greenlease,
Jr., who had theretofore been unlawfully seized, confined, in-
veigled, decoyed, kidnaped, abducted and carried away for ransom,
reward and otherwise, and that the said Robert Cosgrove Greenlease,
Jr., a minor, was not liberated unharmed by the said Carl Austin
Hall and Bonnie Emily Brown Heady.

BUSTING OUT, STAYING OUT

In November 1909 Frank Grigware was convicted of robbing a train carrying U.S. mail near Omaha and sentenced to life imprisonment at the U.S. Penitentiary at Leavenworth. A few months later six Leavenworth prisoners, Grigware among them, jumped a supply train inside the Penitentiary compound and forced the engineer to literally steam their way to freedom through the prison's railroad gate.

Five of the men were recaptured. Grigware remained at large for almost a quarter century. A small "Wanted" card soon was circulated depicting Grigware wearing a bowler hat at a jaunty angle.

In 1934 a Canadian who went by the name of Jim Fahey, hoping to earn money from fur pelts, was cited for trapping out of season. Fahey was a respected citizen of a nearby community and once had served as its mayor. Nevertheless, he was apprehended, Canadian officials took his fingerprints and — following a policy instituted two years earlier — forwarded them to other international law enforcement agencies, including the FBI.

Fahey's prints matched those of Grigware.

In the 1930s the bureau's investigative techniques were constantly growing more sophisticated. One official suggested to director J. Edgar Hoover that the program be expanded to foreign countries and in March 1932, the bureau's international fingerprint exchange program began. In March 1934 it caught Grigware.

To Joe Jackson, author of *Leavenworth Train: A Fugitive's Search for Justice in the Vanishing West*, Grigware's story showcases the blunt end of the American dream at the close of the frontier era. In Jackson's version of events, Grigware left home dreaming of riches from gold mining. But his luck was poor and he proved naïve, falling in with train robbers. Grigware was convicted of participating in the 1909 robbery, Jackson writes, on flimsy evidence.

After Grigware was discovered in 1934, American authorities sought to pursue him but Canada fought extradition. Things continued that way for decades. As late as 1965 officials in the Kansas City FBI kept Grigware's file open on Hoover's request.

In 1977 Grigware died in Canada at age 91, a free man — but not really. Fearing apprehension, he would not attend the funerals of family members in the United States.

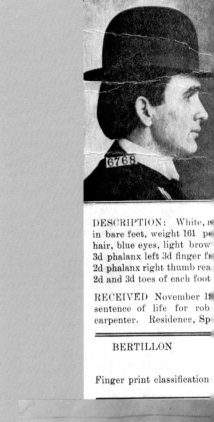

$100 RE

FRANK GRIC

Aliases James Go

Escaped from the
Leavenworth, K

DESCRIPTION: White,
in bare feet, weight 161 p
hair, blue eyes, light brow
3d phalanx left 3d finger f
2d phalanx right thumb rea
2d and 3d toes of each foot

RECEIVED November 1
sentence of life for rob
carpenter. Residence, Sp

BERTILLON

Finger print classification

RD **$100**

RE, No. 6768
E. Hollingshead
tates Penitentiary,
pril 21, 1910.

), height 5 feet 8½ inches
complexion, light brown
r ⅛ inch oblique inner at
scar of ⅛ inch vertical at
t ½ inch below right eye;

Omaha, Nebraska, under
mail train. Occupation,
ngton.

82.0, 93.5, 19.7, 16.4, 14.0,
4, 25.7, 11.5, 9.3, 47.8.

25	10	14
9	00	

UNITED STATES PENITENTIARY,
Leavenworth, Kansas.

Record of _Frank Grigware_   No. 6768

Alias, _James Gordon, E. E. Hollingshead_   Color, _White_

Crime, _Robbing U S Mail Train._

Sentence: _Life_ Years,   Months,   Days. Fine, $: Cost, $ Execution Committed

To date from _Nov 19. 1909_   Convicted, _D of Neb Omaha_

Maximum Term,   Minimum Term,

Received at Penitentiary, _Nov 19. 1909_   Occupation, _Carpenter_ Age, _23_

Escaped Apr 21, 1910. — apprehended in Canada — see letters 5-24-34, Director + 5-12-34 in re withdrawing request for extradition.

DATE	VIOLATIONS.	No. Days in Solitary.	Loss of Days
1910 Jan 4	_Malingering. This man came on sick call this morning claiming diarrhoea. He was placed in quarters for observation with the result that I find he has no dysentery or diarrhoea; but has had only one ordinary passage of bowels, since then (D. Yohe) P. 203._ _Solitary 2.30 P.M. Released Jan 6. 1910. 11. A.m_	2	3

Records from Frank Grigware's brief stay at Leavenworth.
Record Group 129

PRISON MANUSCRIPT

Jack Johnson, the first African-American heavyweight boxing champion, spent several months at the U.S. Penitentiary in Leavenworth in 1921. While there, he began dictating an autobiography that survives as part of his prison file.

Flamboyant and a flouter of that day's social and racial conventions, Johnson constantly attracted attention. He won the heavyweight title in 1908, and in 1912 opened a Chicago nightclub. Often, he was seen in the company of Lucille Cameron, a white secretary.

That year he was charged with violating the Mann Act, which outlawed the interstate transport of women for purposes considered immoral. With those charges facing him, Johnson married Cameron in December 1912. But the next spring, in the federal court of Kenesaw Mountain Landis, future commissioner of baseball, Johnson was convicted.

Freed on appeal, Johnson left the country with Cameron. For several years he traveled the world, earning small purses in boxing and wrestling matches. In 1920 he surrendered to American authorities and was sent to Leavenworth.

Johnson died in a car accident in 1946 and is buried in Chicago.

His career received new attention in 2005 when a documentary by filmmaker Ken Burns, "Unforgivable Blackness: The Rise and Fall of Jack Johnson," aired on public television. That year, believing that the conviction that halted Johnson's career was racially motivated, U. S. Sen. John McCain of Arizona led an effort in Congress to pass legislation for a posthumous presidential pardon.

A draft of Jack Johnson's autobiography, dictated at Leavenworth.
Record Group 129

Life of Jack Johnson

by M C Butler 15509

My mother, Mrs Tiny Johnson, was born in S. C and my father, Mr Henry Johnson was born in N. C. Shortly after their marriage they moved from N. C. to Galveston Tex. It was in that city that I was born on the 31st day of March, 1878. I attended the public schools in Galveston until I reached the age of 12, and until I had reached that age nothing eventful had happened in my life, until that time my life had been simply that of the average school boy. I did not have an older brother to fight my boyhood fights for me, but, I did have an older sister. Her name was Lucy, and Lucy defended me and fought most all my boyhood fights until I became 12 years of age, It was in that year of my life when I first discovered that I could fight just a little bit.

While going home from school one day, I fell into a heated argument with Willie Morris, one of my school mates,

THE BOSS AND THE PRESIDENT

Outside Kansas City, Tom Pendergast's name lives on because of his association with Harry Truman.

The 33rd president began his political career in 1922. Running with the blessing of the Pendergast political organization, he was elected to represent the eastern district of Jackson County, Missouri, as a judge, the title of a county administrator. In 1926 he was elected presiding judge of the county, and he was re-elected in 1930.

Pendergast, meanwhile, dominated the politics of Kansas City and of Jackson County in the 1920s and 1930s and gained a reputation as a skilled yet ruthless machine boss.

Truman worked to maintain a reputation for integrity. Under his leadership, Jackson County voters in 1928 and 1931 approved bond issues for better roads. In 1934 Truman, again representing the Pendergast organization, won election to the U.S. Senate.

As Truman's stock rose, Pendergast's fell.

Pendergast's undoing was horse-racing. Federal investigators found that Pendergast lost $600,000 in 1935 on bad bets. It's cited as one reason that the boss took $440,000 in 1935 and 1936 from insurance companies eager to settle a long-litigated rate case in Missouri.

Federal authorities indicted Pendergast for income-tax evasion in spring 1939. He pleaded guilty and was sentenced to a term in the U.S. Penitentiary in Leavenworth. He was paroled after one year and one day.

To the end, Truman defended Pendergast. Many thought his association with the disgraced boss would scuttle his chances for re-election to the Senate in 1940. But Truman won, and went on to distinguish himself leading a Senate committee investigating war-time defense contracts.

In 1944 Truman was chosen vice presidential candidate for Franklin Roosevelt, who won his fourth term that November.

In January 1945, when Truman had been vice president for only days, Pendergast died of coronary disease. Truman flew from Washington to Kansas City to attend Pendergast's funeral. Less than three months later, Roosevelt died, and Truman was sworn in as president.

Pendergast seeks more time to repay taxes.
Record Group 21

4

THE DISTRICT COURT OF THE UNITED STATES FOR THE WESTERN DIVISION
OF THE WESTERN DISTRICT OF MISSOURI.

NITED STATES OF AMERICA,	)
Plaintiff,	)
vs.	) No. 14,567
THOMAS J. PENDERGAST,	)
Defendant.	)

**MOTION OF DEFENDANT, THOMAS J. PENDERGAST,
FOR ENLARGEMENT OF PERIOD FIXED BY CONDITIONS
OF PROBATION WITHIN WHICH TO PAY REMAINING
UNPAID INTEREST ON TAX LIABILITIES.**

Comes now the defendant, Thomas J. Pendergast, and
ates that the terms and conditions upon which probation was
posed included, among others, a provision reading as follows:

"3.   The defendant will promptly pay to the
United States of America the full amount, with
legal penalties, of all income taxes which have
been or may be assessed against him for the two
years referred to in this indictment, unless,
before the period of probation begins, he
already has paid such amounts; provided, however,
that it will not be considered to be a violation
of this condition if the defendant pays less than
the full amounts assessed, through any concession
or waiver made by the taxing authorities of the
United States; and, provided further that probation will not be revoked for failure to
comply with this condition if it shall be proved
to the court that the defendant is not financially
able to comply with the condition and that he was
not financially able to pay the taxes due on the
date the indictment in this case was returned."

fendant further states that immediately after sentence was
posed in the within case negotiations were started with the
easury Department, with the view of determining immediately the
ture and extent of defendant's liability or claimed liability

STATE OF MISSOURI   )
) SS
COUNTY OF JACKSON   )

Thomas J. Pendergast, of lawful age, first being duly
sworn, upon his oath states that he has read the foregoing Motion,
is familiar with the facts and matters therein contained, and that
said facts are true to his best knowledge and belief.

T. J. Pendergast

Subscribed and sworn to before me this 26 day of
August, 1941.

Ruth Toward Moore
Notary Public.

My Commission expires June 7, 1945.

Birth of the FBI

Today the events of June 17, 1933, outside Kansas City's Union Station are known as the Union Station Massacre. What happened there that day had vast consequences not only in Kansas City but across the country.

Four lawmen, plus a gangster named Frank Nash, died in an exchange of gunfire that broke out as the authorities escorted Nash through the crowded train station to return him by car to Leavenworth penitentiary.

According to Robert Unger, a former *Kansas City Times* and *Star* reporter who in 1997 published *The Union Station Massacre: the Original Sin of J. Edgar Hoover's FBI*, the modern Federal Bureau of Investigation can be traced to that event.

The deaths in Kansas City, Unger wrote, punctured the popular perception of gangsters. Before that day the bandits were considered misunderstood country boys, christened with headline-friendly names such as "Pretty Boy" or "Baby Face." Often in their exploits, they embarrassed lawmen around the heartland.

The savagery of the deaths in Kansas City changed all that, and J. Edgar Hoover saw an opportunity.

At the time, Hoover was struggling to get money for his fledgling Bureau of Investigation, then just another division of the Justice Department. The shootout at Kansas City's Union Station occurred only a few months after the inauguration of President Franklin Roosevelt. By June 1934, Roosevelt had signed nine anti-crime bills into law, creating a new federal criminal code. The bills made federal offenses of transporting kidnapping victims or stolen property over state lines, and soon expanded the crime-fighting jurisdiction of Hoover's bureau.

Yet the lack of a conviction in the Union Station matter frustrated Hoover. Soon after the event, he wrote his agents that those responsible for the massacre "must be exterminated and they must be exterminated by us."

One candidate was Adam Richetti, a sidekick of gangster Charles "Pretty Boy" Floyd. According to legend, Floyd was thought to have been present at the shootings, but others have cast doubt on that. However, agents soon began circling Richetti. They fingered him for being present at Union Station, contradicting confidential reports they had made to Hoover earlier. Also, Unger found, they watched ballistics data they deemed questionable entered into evidence against Richetti in his 1935 trial in Kansas City.

Eventually Richetti was found guilty of killing one of the two Kansas City detectives who died in the massacre. In 1938 Richetti became the first to die in the new gas chamber in the Missouri State Penitentiary.

Outside Kansas City's Union Station, a crowd quickly gathered at the scene of the shootout, where bodies and broken glass still lay. *Non-record material from Federal Bureau of Investigation, Central Plains Region branch.*

BALL GAMES AT THE BIG HOUSE

William G. Wilson, better known in his time as "Baseball" Wilson, helped bring the sport to Leavenworth penitentiary.

Wilson made his big league debut in 1890 with the Pittsburgh Alleghenys of the National League, and played about 10 years of professional baseball at various levels. In 1910, after he arrived at Leavenworth, a beer distributor in Omaha, Nebraska, sent Wilson a baseball bat — with a letter assuring prison authorities that the club was meant only for baseball.

At one time, the idea would have been outlandish. Over the years, Leavenworth officials worried about security, sometimes forbidding the prisoners even to speak to one another.

But Wilson's baseball bat arrived about the time officials began allowing yard privileges to prisoners. Soon baseball was being played. Then it was organized. Separate teams consisted of white players, whose team was called the Brown Sox; African-Americans, whose team was named the Booker T. Washingtons, and American Indians, who named their team the Red Men.

One-time heavyweight boxing champion Jack Johnson sometimes umpired the games, suggesting that few players wanted to dispute his judgment of balls and strikes.

Organized baseball endured at Leavenworth through the 1960s.

Why was "Baseball" Wilson at Leavenworth in the first place? He was convicted of forging postal money orders, and sentenced by federal judge Kenesaw Mountain Landis. Later, Landis became the first commissioner of baseball and is remembered for banning from baseball eight members of the Chicago White Sox accused of throwing the 1919 World Series.

"Baseball" Wilson and the letter sent to prison officials by Blatz Beer's representative.
Record Group 129

Wilson

Omaha, Neb., Nov 24th 1910

United States Penitentiary
Leavenworth, Kas

Gentlemen,-

To-day I expressed a Box to one of your prisoners by the name William Wilson Reg No 6636- and overlooked paying the charges at this end.

I am enclosing you 50 cts. in stamps which I trust will pay charges, Hoping this will not inconvenience you to much and thanking you in advance for your trouble I am

Yours Resp.

M. J. Gibson

SEASON'S GREETINGS — PRISON BARS OR NO

nce you entered federal prison, your personal life became public property.

Authorities at Leavenworth logged incoming mail and telegrams, too — among them colorful ones devised by Western Union for the Christmas holidays.

There's the telegram from the spouse or girlfriend of inmate Tim Murphy, who dreamed that bad times soon would be behind them. There's also the telegram from the parents of Vincent Michael O'Brien, whose imprisonment didn't deter them from mentioning how proud they'd been that he served as an altar boy at Christmas mass.

Files of some Leavenworth prisoners include Christmas cards sent to the penitentiary after the prisoner had left — suggesting a parolee who wanted to remain on good terms with prison officials.

Those officials also maintained records of seasonal gifts received by inmates. Especially popular items: calendars.

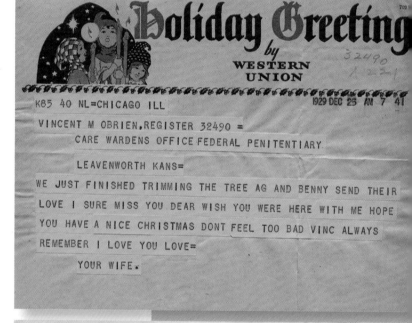

Holiday Greeting by WESTERN UNION

K85 40 NL=CHICAGO ILL   1929 DEC 25 AM 7 41

VINCENT M OBRIEN, REGISTER 32490 =
   CARE WARDENS OFFICE FEDERAL PENITENTIARY

LEAVENWORTH KANS=

WE JUST FINISHED TRIMMING THE TREE AG AND BENNY SEND THEIR
LOVE I SURE MISS YOU DEAR WISH YOU WERE HERE WITH ME HOPE
YOU HAVE A NICE CHRISTMAS DONT FEEL TOO BAD VINC ALWAYS
REMEMBER I LOVE YOU LOVE=
      YOUR WIFE.

Holiday Greeting WESTERN UNION TELEGRAM

60K RN 15

      TE CLEVELAND OHIO 231P JAN 1 1925

TIM MURPHY

      FEDERAL PRISON LEAVENWORTH KANS

HOPE THIS NEW YEAR WILL BE A HAPPYER ONE FOR BOTH OF US WITH LOVE

            FLORENCE

                  319P

Cheery Christmas telegrams for inmate Tim Murphy, right, and Vincent O'Brien, above. Right: O'Brien's record.
Record Group 129

UNITED STATES PENITENTIARY
LEAVENWORTH, KANSAS

Name Vincent O'Brien   Register No. 32490   Color White

Alias Michael O'Brien, Morris O'Brien.

Crime Robbery of Mail with Firearms & Conspiracy

Received   May 25 1929   From ND-Illinois:Chicago

Sentence   15 Years.   Fine, costs, etc. --

Date of Sentence   May 20 1929   Sentence begins   May 25 1929

Maximum term expires May 24 1944   Minimum term expires   June 20 1939

Good time allowed   1800   days.   Eligible for parole   May 24 1934

Civil or Military   Civil   Occupation Book-Kepper   Age 26

Where arrested Chicago,Ill   . When Apr 16 1929

How long in jail before trial since arrest   Nativity Illinois.

How long in U. S. life   Citizen of U. S. yes

Father living? yes   Mother living? yes

Name of Father Micheal O'Brien   Name of Mother   Bridget O'Brien

Present address of parents 4517 Lake Park,Chicago,Ill.

Nativity of Father Illinois   Nativity of Mother Illinois

Married yes   Wife living yes   Children   Boys

Wife's name and present address Marie O'Brien,4517 Lake Park,Chicago

Your residence Illinois,Chicago,

In case of sickness or death, notify Wife,see above

Education: Read yes   Write yes   Common school 6   High sch

Religion Catholic   Preference

Chew tobacco no   . Smoke yes   Drink yes   Use Opium or Morphine no

Ex-Service Man

(OVER)

A PRISON GALLERY

STRIKING TERROR IN 1916

LEAVENWORTH WON'T TAKE HER

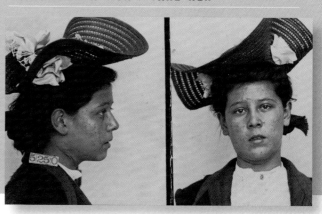

The torch of the Statue of Liberty in New York has been closed to visitors since 1916.

That could be the legacy of Lothar Witzke, a native of Germany who was convicted as a spy in World War I. Some federal authorities believed he was complicit in the Black Tom Island explosion of July 30, 1916, which blew up 1,000 tons of munitions awaiting shipment to Europe, and killed seven people. The Statue of Liberty, about a mile from Black Tom Island, was damaged in the blast and the torch closed as a result.

About 18 months later, after the United States had declared war on Germany, federal authorities arrested Witzke near the Mexican border. In August 1918 a military commission at Fort Sam Houston, Texas, convicted him of collecting information about Army troops, and sentenced him to be hanged. President Woodrow Wilson commuted the sentence to life imprisonment at hard labor.

In May 1920 authorities delivered him to Leavenworth. He was discharged in 1923 and returned to Germany.

Lizzie Cardish was convicted of arson in Wisconsin and sentenced to life imprisonment on June 12, 1906. She arrived at Leavenworth three days later. That's when the warden realized his new inmate was female.

Nobody had told him and — as he soon wrote federal authorities in Washington — he had no place to put her that would keep her at a safe remove from the male prisoners.

Another thing: Lizzie was 15. She was "a mere child, frightened at her surroundings, nervous and badly needing the care of a woman," the warden wrote.

He transferred her the next day to the Kansas state prison in Lansing, just south of Leavenworth, saying:

"Her immediate transfer to the female department of the Kansas State Prison was an act rendered necessary by the highest considerations of propriety and, indeed, humanity."

Lizzie Cardish stayed at Lansing the rest of the summer. That September, after she received a presidential commutation of her sentence, authorities transferred her to the Illinois State Training School for Girls in Geneva, Illinois.

A PRISON PREVIEW

BUSTED FOR MARIJUANA

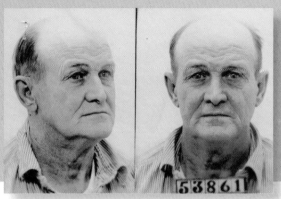

Lemuel Hawkins got his first look at Leavenworth 1922 as a member of the Kansas City Monarchs, which agreed to play the prison's African-American baseball team, the Booker T. Washingtons.

In 1931, Hawkins saw what Leavenworth was like from the inside. That year, police in Chanute, Kansas, arrested him for auto theft. He was sentenced to two years in the penitentiary for violating the Dyer Act, passed in 1919 to fight the interstate transport of stolen cars.

Hawkins arrived at Leavenworth in November, and soon signed up to play baseball. He was released in summer 1933.

The Marijuana Tax Act of 1937 made the substance illegal in the United States.

It didn't take long for Samuel Caldwell to find himself in federal prison for violating the act. He arrived at Leavenworth penitentiary in October 1937, soon after being sentenced to a minimum of two years. Archivists at the Central Plains Region believe Caldwell was the first prisoner convicted under the marijuana act to arrive at Leavenworth.

Prison officials didn't seem too worried about Caldwell, who at 57 had served various sentences in state and federal prisons for offenses such as burglary, issuing fraudulent checks and violating various liquor and narcotics laws. Documents quoted Caldwell as saying this sentence represented just another "bit behind bars." One official noted that it was an experience "to which he is inured from much previous experience."

Describing Caldwell as a "persistent violator," authorities also recorded that he was "cheerful, well liked by others, well balanced." In 1939 Caldwell was sent to another federal institution, McNeil Island in Washington state, to relieve crowding at Leavenworth.

M.D. HALL FARM
ALFALFA HAY FROM 1/3 ACRE

EROSION

THIEF OF THE FIELDS!

EROSION HAS TAKEN MORE THAN A TON OF SOIL FOR EVERY BUSHEL OF CORN AND GRAIN GROWN ON SLOPING LAND.

IA-50.068

5.

GOVERNMENT GEARS UP

More than 50,000 cubic feet of documents are filed at the Central Plains Region branch and much of it details the work of more than 90 federal agencies in Iowa, Missouri, Kansas, Minnesota and Nebraska, as well as North and South Dakota. The files show how the federal government tried to respond to complex and challenging issues, such as flood control in the southern Mississippi River Valley in the 1920s, or urban housing needs in St. Louis after World War II.

FINDING WORK

The Civilian Conservation Corps was one of President Franklin Roosevelt's first initiatives to fight unemployment during the Depression. As its name implied, a major part of its job was conservation of natural resources.

The Emergency Conservation Work Act, or ECW — more commonly known as the Civilian Conservation Corps, or CCC — enrolled more than 3.4 million young men from 1933 through 1942.

About 1,600 camps operated in the United States each year. Sometimes their operators produced yearbooks, like the one chronicling life in a CCC camp in Butler, Missouri, from November 1, 1935, through April 1, 1936. It shows how the young men often lived in barracks, had access to a camp exchange and library, and labored over diversion ditches and other soil conservation measures using horse-drawn implements.

On the front lines with the CCC, above, moving rocks and around camp, right.
Record Group 114

SAVING THE SOIL

In the 1930s and 1940s, the federal government devoted time and attention to soil conservation, often in cooperation with states.

Various farming techniques were promoted to discourage erosion. For example: to avoid heavy loss of soil in late summer and fall rains, plant a cover of rye between rows of crops. The rye served as a soil binder.

Today the black-and-white photographs that accompanied the conservation suggestions recall the Farm Security Administration series of Depression-era photographs documenting the desperation of migrant workers and the sometimes ruined lands they encountered. Many of the soil conservation photographs, though, convey a hopeful, more upbeat message.

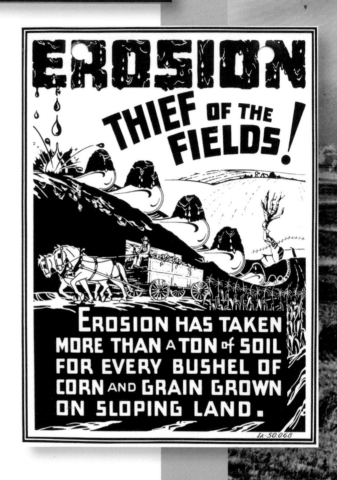

Government posters warned of the threat of erosion, and pictures tried to show how properly managed fields were productive fields.

Record Group 114

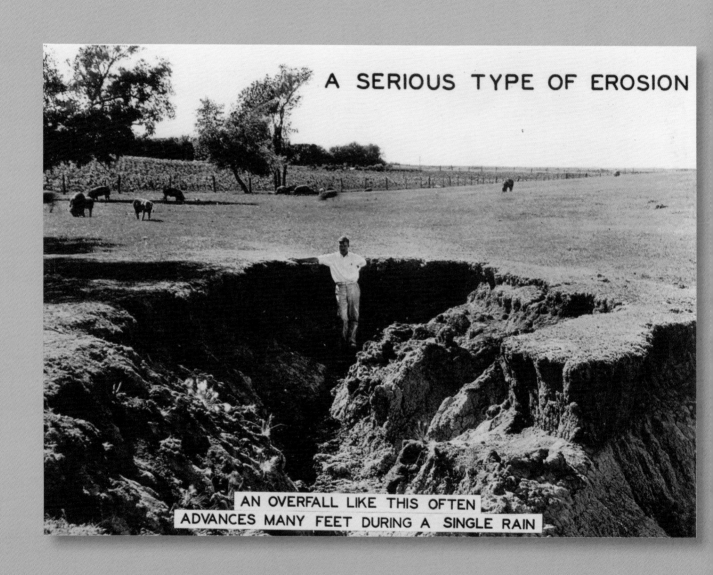

A SERIOUS TYPE OF EROSION

AN OVERFALL LIKE THIS OFTEN
ADVANCES MANY FEET DURING A SINGLE RAIN

PERMANENTLY CONTROLLED

WATER FLOWING OVER THIS ROCK MASONRY
DAM FALLS HARMLESSLY ON A LOOSE ROCK APRON

1922-1

114·SC·MO·81

MO-1308 - Bessie Parker farm, Leon, Iowa Project
Mo-1, 2/2/39.   The erosion in these fields has
reduced the value of the farm to the point where all
but 40 acres have been taken over for taxes.   The
remaining 40 will be taken over sometime this year,
unless, of course, the back taxes are paid.   The
farm was originally composed of 160 acres, selling
in 1875 for $6.00 per acre.   The land increased in
value to a maximum in 1916 when the 40 acres sold
for $1,500.   The present owner purchased this 40 acres
for $47.00 per acre in 1928.   The land changed hands
twenty-two times during this period and was reduced
from a 160-acre unit to a 40-acre unit and then increased to its present size of 63 acres.   The taxes
on the 40 acres for 1938 was $30.00.   See Mo-1309
and 1310.

ALFALFA HAY FROM ⅓ ACRE

GOOD INTENTIONS, POOR RESULT

If the phrase "housing project" rings like a pejorative these days, one likely reason is the Pruitt-Igoe project in St. Louis, completed in 1956.

The two names given to the federally funded project were meant to generate regional pride. Capt. Wendell Oliver Pruitt was an African-American fighter pilot from St. Louis who died in World War II. U.S. Rep. William L. Igoe served several terms in Congress before and after World War I, representing the congressional district in which the project was built.

But today their combined names live on as bitter shorthand for well-intentioned social engineering gone wrong on a vast scale.

The more than 30 buildings of Pruitt-Igoe were meant to rehabilitate a district on the near north side of St. Louis. The buildings were considered a new approach to urban living. In 1951 the publication *Architectural Forum* praised the project's "refreshing" site plan and a landscaping design that called for a minimum of 200 feet between buildings and a park "stretched out to wind through the area like a river."

It just didn't work out.

"Children were exposed to crime and drug use, despite the attempts of their parents to provide a positive environment," recalled *The St. Louis Post-Dispatch* in 2004. "No one felt ownership of the green spaces that were designed as recreational areas, so no one took care of them. A mini-city of 10,000 people was stacked into an environment of despair."

Minoru Yamasaki, one of the project architects, believed the project was just too big. The original concept called for garden apartments interspersed with high-rise towers, but public housing officials apparently persuaded Yamasaki to almost double the density. It wound up with 2,870 apartments.

Over the years, designers kept trying. Site plans show how outdoor areas were being fine-tuned as late as 1964.

Eventually federal authorities conceded defeat. One toured Pruitt-Igoe in 1970 after visiting an equally infamous housing project in Chicago.

"My tour of Cabrini-Green last week was still quite fresh in my mind," wrote the federal housing official in November 1970. "There is no comparison. Pruitt-Igoe is the second most devastated set of buildings I have ever seen. It is exceeded only in my experience by the bombed out buildings in Japan and Korea, but not by very much. Most of the buildings in the complex hardly had a window left intact."

By 1973 the sentiments captured in Housing and Urban Development correspondence were candid. It was essential that the housing project be razed, read one 1973 internal memo, "because of the stigma that has become attached to the project and its name."

Beginning in the early 1970s, the buildings were imploded.

Aerial photos were used to show how Pruitt-Igoe looked overall. Through the years, landscaping improvements couldn't save the project.
Record Group 196

MINDING THE MISSISSIPPI

Controversy over natural disaster preparedness in New Orleans is not a recent phenomenon.

The Mississippi River Commission was established by Congress as early as 1879 to oversee federal funds for flood control. In 1922 the president of the New Orleans Association of Commerce wrote President Warren Harding asking that a new river commission be seated to study flood control from a fresh perspective.

A sharp debate followed. Officials from Greenville, Mississippi, north of New Orleans, were adamant in their preference for the continued building of levees, as often practiced by the river commission.

Still other ideas were floated. A 1925 map detailed a flood relief plan that would introduce spillways into various basins in the district.

All this came before the April 1927 flood that devastated several states in the southern Mississippi River valley. Greenville was inundated, and became one of several Mississippi river communities that housed refugees in tents.

Scholars believe the flood helped Huey Long become governor of Louisiana in 1928. That same year Congress approved the National Flood Control Act.

The event also is thought to have prompted what often is called the Great Migration of African-Americans from the Mississippi Delta region to points north, Chicago chief among them. From 1920 to 1930, the African-American population of Chicago increased from 109,458 to 233,903.

One plan for controlling flooding along the Mississippi.
Record Group 77

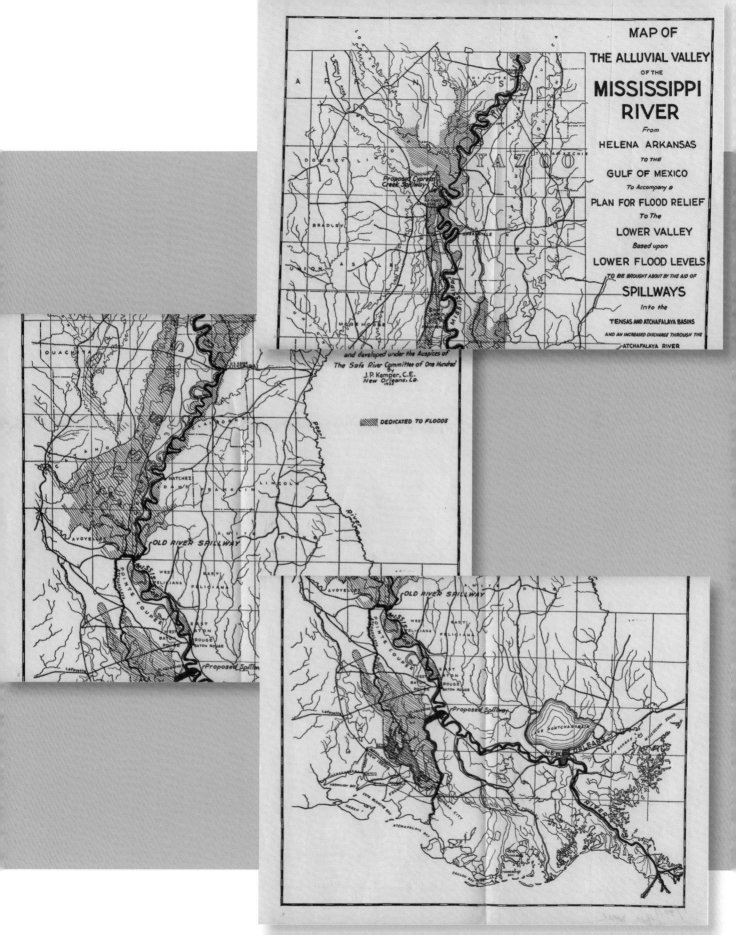

MAP OF
THE ALLUVIAL VALLEY
OF THE
MISSISSIPPI
RIVER
From
HELENA ARKANSAS
TO THE
GULF OF MEXICO
To Accompany a
PLAN FOR FLOOD RELIEF
To The
LOWER VALLEY
Based upon
LOWER FLOOD LEVELS
TO BE BROUGHT ABOUT BY THE AID OF
SPILLWAYS
Into the
TENSAS AND ATCHAFALAYA BASINS
AND AN INCREASED DISCHARGE THROUGH THE
ATCHAFALAYA RIVER

and developed under the Auspices of
The Safe River Committee of One Hundred
by
J.P. Kemper, C.E.
New Orleans, La.
1928

DEDICATED TO FLOODS

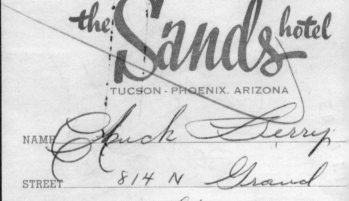

No. 801   MAY 4, 1912   5 CENTS

NICK CARTER
WEEKLY

THE RED BUTTON

STREET & SMITH
PUBLISHERS
NEW YORK

the **Sands** hotel

TUCSON - PHOENIX, ARIZONA

NAME *Chuck Berry*

STREET *814 N Grand*

CITY and STATE *St Louis N*
For Your Protection Please Give Full Address

MAKE
OF CAR _____ LICENSE
NUMBER _____ STATE _____

REPRESENTING _____

NOTICE TO GUESTS
A safe is provided for the deposit of money and jewelry. T
for valuables not deposited

IN THE UNITED STATES DISTRICT COURT FOR THE

DISTRICT OF NEBRASKA

FILED
DISTRICT OF NEBRASKA
AT _____
MAR 8 1963
Richard P. Peck C
By _____ De

UNITED STATES OF AMERICA,	)	
Plaintiff,	)	CR. 0753
vs.	)	
NICHOLAS KING NOLTE,	)	JUDGMENT AND
Defendant.	)	ORDER OF PROBATION

On March 7, 1963, came the attorney for the United

States, Frederic J. Coufal, Assistant United States Attorney

The handwritten hotel receipt/card on the left:

BERRY

Nº 51145

ATE 12/2

OON 256-257

EP. DATE 12/3

O. GUESTS 4

ATE 22⁰⁰

OLIO 5145

ERK WOM

not be responsible

KAYCO SPECIAL

6.

IN COURT: A ROCKY ROAD TO FAME, DEFENDING TURF AND OTHER BATTLES

In the files of the District Courts of the United States, you'll find familiar names under unfamiliar circumstances. In one, there's the record of a young and bankrupt Walt Disney in the early 1920s. In another are details on Omaha resident Nick Nolte, young and in trouble in the early 1960s for distributing fake Selective Service applications. That occurred about a decade and a half before he achieved celebrity as an actor. Sometimes supporting evidence is far more striking than the case itself. One file is replete with pictures of huge movie displays for Harold Lloyd, Clara Bow and Douglas Fairbanks. The pictures also documented the 1920s urban streetscape around the theater — all used in a fight over retail competition.

HIS SONG, HIS PROPERTY

"If music did not pay, it would be given up."

So wrote Justice Oliver Wendell Holmes Jr. of the U.S. Supreme Court in a 1917 opinion. It affirmed that copyright law protected composers from hotel and restaurant owners who used music without compensating the writer.

In 1927, the owner of a restaurant in rural Jackson County, Missouri, learned about this the hard way. That September, documents were served on the restaurateur, William C. Glover, alerting him that he had been named in a complaint brought by no less than Irving Berlin.

Berlin, perhaps the most famous songwriter in America, was joined in the complaint by Gene Buck, president of the American Society of Composers, Authors and Publishers.

The society was formed in 1914 to protect royalties due songwriters for public performances of their compositions. Three years later, the Supreme Court upheld the suit of an ASCAP founding member, songwriter Victor Herbert, against the owners of a New York restaurant. They had refused to pay royalties for a Herbert melody performed by the restaurant's mechanical player piano.

One of ASCAP's enthusiastic early members was Berlin.

He charged that Glover, owner of Beautiful Wildwood Lakes on Woodson Road a mile southeast of Raytown, had featured performances of "Russian Lullaby," which Berlin wrote. The complaint also said Glover had used "Me and My Shadow," not a Berlin composition but one for which his music publishing company held the copyright.

It was no contest.

The complaint was issued in September. In November, Albert Reeves, a federal judge in Kansas City, sided with Berlin and Buck. He ordered Glover to pay court costs and warned him that the plaintiffs could take similar actions in the future.

GENE BUCK, as President of the American Society
of Composers, Authors and Publishers, and
IRVING BERLIN, INC., A Corporation,

Plaintiffs,

In Equity

against

WILLIAM C. GLOVER,

Defendant .

FIRST COUNT.

The /complaint of the plaintiffs allege that at all the times hereinafter
mentioned:

I. That the plaintiff, American Society of Composers, Authors and
Publishers, (hereinafter referred to, for brevity's sake, as the "Society"),
at all the times hereinafter mentioned, was and still is an unincorporated
association, consisting of more than seven members, duly organized and
existing under the Laws of the State of New York, and that said Gene
Buck is the President thereof. That the Society at all such times was
and still is composed of authors, composers and publishers of musical
works and was organized for the purpose of protecting the performing
rights in their musical works against infringement. That the principal
place of business of said Society is in the Borough of Manhattan, City of
New York, in the Southern District of New York.

II. That the pla[...]
(hereinafter for brevi[...]
hereinafter mentioned[...]
under the laws of the[...]
business in the Borou[...]
District of New York[...]
still is engaged in th[...]
copyrighted musical v[...]

III. That the de[...]
was   a[...]
resident of this d[...]

IV. Upon inform[...]
mentioned, the defendant owned, controlled, managed and operated, and
still own, manage, control, and operate a certain place of public entertainment, accommodation and refreshment, known as Beautiful Wildwood
Lakes
ocated at Woodson Road, 1¼ miles southeast of Raytown,
n the City of County of Jackson
n the State of Missouri
n this District. That for the entertainment and amusement of the
patrons attending such place, daily performances and renditions of

The action filed by Berlin and
ASCAP.
Record Group 21

V. That prior to the 10th day of   May   19 27 ,
7   Billy Rose   , citizen   of the United States, originated,
devised, created and wrote the words and lyrics of a new and original
musical composition, and that also prior to the said date,
Asa Yoelson and Dave Dreyer   ,   citizens of the United States,
composed and set original music to the said words and lyrics, and the
said words and lyrics, together with the said music, constituted a musical
composition, entitled "ME AND MY SHADOW"

VI. That prior to the 10th day of   May   19 27 ,
8   the said author s and composer s assigned such composition to the
Publisher, including all rights therein, and the right to secure copyright therein.

He plays the guitar, your honor

Forty years before the Kennedy Center gave Chuck Berry its lifetime achievement award in 2000, federal authorities prosecuted him for violating the Mann Act.

They accused him of taking an underage Native American woman from Texas to Missouri for immoral purposes. Berry said he had hired the woman to work as a hostess at his nightclub in St. Louis. He had been told she was 21, he said.

By the time of the trial, Berry was nationally famous. Yet transcripts from *United States v. Charles Edward Anderson Berry* suggest that Berry's lawyer thought he had to lead the jury as if by hand through the mysteries of rock 'n' roll.

Q. What kind of entertaining do you do?
A. I do personal engagements, singing and playing an instrument.

Q. What instrument do you play?
A. Guitar.

Prosecutors, meanwhile, grilled Berry on the details of his sleeping habits while on tour with his band. They asked how and when he used the bed in his hotel rooms as he traveled with the woman to St. Louis.

Q. Was it still your intention to sleep the next day?
A. To sleep the next day?

Q. Yes.
A. Yes, sir, it was my intention.

Q. I can't hear you, Mr. Berry.

Berry's account of the prosecution in his 1987 autobiography directs frustration not so much at the prosecutors as at the newspaper reporters who incorporated lyrics from Berry songs such as "Sweet Little Sixteen" in their accounts of the trial.

He was convicted and reported to authorities in February 1962. Berry lived at federal institutions in Terre Haute, Indiana; Springfield, Missouri, and Leavenworth — where he gave a concert. By then, he had learned that "rock" constituted a despised word inside the penitentiary's stone walls.

At Springfield he earned a high school equivalency diploma. Among his courses was typing. He also had plenty of time to write songs, one of which was "No Particular Place to Go."

Authorities released Berry in October 1963. In a way, he felt some of the time had been well spent.

"It may be odd to some but I've always believed that no place or condition can really hinder a person from being free if he has an active, imaginative mind," he wrote. "There is one thing for sure, I did cheat the government of my imprisonment by way of the achievements I accomplished while there. Sorry, great white father, you can't indict me for that."

UNITED STATES DISTRICT COURT
EASTERN DISTRICT OF MISSOURI
EASTERN DIVISION

FILED

JUN 10 1960

GEO. J. BRENNAN
Clerk

NITED STATES OF AMERICA)
)
vs.) No. 59 CR 322
)
HARLES EDWARD ANDERSON BERRY,) Co
)
Defendant.)

        Transcript of proceedi   23
dduced during trial of the above-styl
aving started on February 29, 1960, a
ay to day, as shown herein.

        ___

Vol. 1

Pages 1 - 211.

VOL.2

Excerpts from the rock 'n' roller's
testimony: "Four of my records have
sold over a million copies, sir."
Record Group 21

AFTERNOON SESSION

        The Court: You may proceed.

        CHARLES EDWARD ANDERSON BERRY,

was called as a witness, and being first duly sworn to

tell the truth, the whole truth and nothing but the truth,

testified as follows:

                DIRECT EXAMINATION

                        By Mr. Silverstein

Q   What is your name, please?

A   Charles Edward Anderson Berry.

Q   And are you also known as Chuck Berry?

A   Yes sir.

Q   Where do you live, sir?

A   13 Windemere Place, St. Louis, Missouri.

Q   How old are you?

A   Thirty-three.

Q   When were you born?

A   October 18, 1926.

Q   Are you a married man?

A   Yes, I am.

Q   How long have you been married?

A   Eleven years and some months.

Q   What is the date of your marriage?

A   October 28, 1948.

HE PLAYS THE GUITAR, YOUR HONOR

that conviction?

A   Just past eighteen, sir.   Sorry, just past seventeen, sir.

Q   Did you enter a plea of guilty?

A   Yes sir, I did.

Q   As a result of that conviction did you serve any time in any correctional institution?

A   Yes sir, I did.

Q   What institution was that?

A   The Intermediate Reformatory for Young Men, Algoa.

Q   How long did you serve there, sir?

A   Three years and a few days, sir.

Q   What is your present occupation, Mr. Berry?

A   I am an entertainer, song writer.

Q   Do you play a musical instrument?

A   Yes sir.

Q   What musical instrument is that?

A   It is a guitar, sir.

Q   How long have you been playing a guitar, participating in music?

A   I have handled the guitar for some ten years. I have been playing professionally for some five years.

Q   Had you ever taken professional lessons?

A   Only out of a book, sir, if that is professional.

Berry - direct

Q   Now, in the year 1959, at the present time, were you
and are you now still engaged in the entertainment field?

A   Yes sir, I am.

Q   And what various media of the entertainment field
have you been participating in?

A   I am sorry.   I don't know what a media means.

Q   What branches of the entertainment field?

A   I am a television artist, that is I have appeared on
television, radio.   I have recorded records.   I have
made personal appearances throughout the country and a few
abroad.

Q   Have you on your own made a number of recordings?

A   Yes sir, forty-seven to be exact.

Q   And have any of these been what you would call in the
business successful recordings?

A   Yes sir.

Q   Did any sell over a million copies?

A   Four of my records have sold over a million copies,
sir.

Q   Have you also written songs, lyrics and music that were
published?

A   Yes sir.   I have had the opportunity to write all of
the songs I have recorded.

Q   In other words, all the songs you have recorded are

POOR AS A MOUSE

Like a lot of small-business owners, Walt Disney had cash flow problems.

In May 1922, he established his first animation business, Laugh-O-gram Films Inc., in Kansas City. In December 1923, the first meeting of creditors convened in Laugh-O-gram's bankruptcy.

What went wrong?

As the Laugh-O-gram bankruptcy files at the Central Plains Region suggest — and as Disney acknowledged — he paid too little attention to the business side of animation.

A few months after starting Laugh-O-gram, Disney signed an agreement to deliver six animated fairy tales to the Tennessee branch of Pictorial Clubs Inc., a film distribution company that catered to schools and churches. The company sent Disney a check for $100 and promised $11,000 for the finished six films.

The animator's problem: The $11,000 wasn't due until Jan. 1, 1924.

Meanwhile, Disney had expenses, and bankruptcy documents detailed how thin Disney's resources were spread.

He had credit accounts with hardware stores and other suppliers. He had payroll; several young animators earned $25 a week.

He rented several rooms at the McConahy Building at 31st Street and Forest Avenue in Kansas City. He also used the message service offered by the Kansas City Telephone Co. That cost a few dollars a month on top of the $15 monthly service fee.

Things went south in a hurry. First, Pictorial Clubs declared bankruptcy. In January 1923, Disney faced a complaint about unpaid rent.

The next month, hardware store owner Fred Schmeltz loaned Laugh-O-gram $500 in exchange for three sets of motion picture lights. On June 2, Schmeltz forwarded $750 more in exchange for nearly every Laugh-O-gram asset not nailed down, including one rolltop desk, one filing cabinet, one hat rack, four steel wastebaskets and two cuspidors.

It still wasn't enough.

So Disney made a dental hygiene film for a local dentist. He also filmed Kansas City children for their parents.

Yet bankruptcy arrived anyway. At their first meeting, Laugh-O-gram creditors tallied up what Disney owed. Animator Ub Iwerks, one of Disney's best friends, claimed he was owed $1,003 in back pay. Franz Wurm Hardware and Paint Co., two blocks from Laugh-O-gram offices on East 31st Street, kept track of every shim (10 cents) and hose connection (20 cents) that Laugh-O-gram had bought on credit. Wurm's list totaled $38.23.

Schutte Lumber Co. of Kansas City wanted $42.27. The Kansas City Telephone Co. sought $39.57.

The bankruptcy case finally was resolved in 1927. Creditors recovered about 45 percent of the money they claimed.

As much as the Disney bankruptcy attests to poor business practice, it also testifies to his considerable charm.

Barely in his 20s and with only one year of high school when he set out, Disney persuaded many friends and acquaintances to contribute about $15,000 to establish Laugh-O-gram. Adjusted for inflation, that would be worth more than $150,000 today.

Even after his stumble, animators stuck with him. Iwerks became one of Disney's chief collaborators. Today he is remembered as the animator perhaps most responsible for the early renderings of Mickey Mouse. That character, which revived Disney's career in the late 1920s, was based on a mouse that had visited Disney during the young artist's lean days at the Laugh-O-gram offices.

Disney left Kansas City in summer 1923 for California, where he would try again — and this time succeed.

Notice of First Meeting of Creditors.

In the District Court of the United States for the Western Division of the Western District of Missouri.
IN BANKRUPTCY.

IN THE MATTER OF

Laugh-O-Gram Films, Inc.,

> In Bankruptcy.

Bankrupt.

To the Creditors of.........Laugh-O-Gram Films, Inc.,.........

of.........Kansas City,.........in the County of *Jackson, and District aforesaid, Bankrupt:*

Notice is hereby given that on the.........30th.........day of.........October,.........A. D. 1923, the said Laugh-O-Gram Films, Inc.,

.... was duly adjudicated bankrupt; and that the first meeting of his creditors will be held at room 300 Fidelity Trust Building, at Kansas City, Missouri, or the.........3rd.........day of.........December;.........A. D. 1923, at ten o'clock in the forenoon, at which time the said creditors may attend, prove their claims, appoint a trustee, examine the bankrupt, and transact such other business as may properly come before said meeting; the said meeting to be held at Kansas City, as the meeting of creditors at Independence, the county seat, would be manifestly inconvenient for the parties in interest, and the said meeting is held at Kansas City in pursuance of an order of the District Court of the United States.

ELMER N. POWELL,

Kansas City, Mo.,.........November 20th 1923. Referee in Bankruptcy.

NOTICE:—Prove your claim, in form as provided by the Bankrupt Law, at once. Attach original note or itemized account.

From Walt Disney's bankruptcy file.
Record Group 21

CITY, MO., November 30 192 3

AFTER DATE We PROMISE

10 — — — — — — — — — — — — — — — — DOLLARS

AS CITY, MISSOURI, FOR VALUE RECEIVED, WITH INTEREST

X PER CENT PER ANNUM. ALL ENDORSERS AND PARTIES

Laugh-O-gram Films Inc.
Walter E Disney President

IN COLD BLOOD REVISITED

Few murders have been more closely examined than the killing of four members of the Clutter family in Holcomb, Kansas, in November 1959.

Two men, Richard Hickock and Perry Edward Smith, were convicted of that crime the following March. The story has grown familiar through the 1966 publication of *In Cold Blood,* an account of the murders by writer Truman Capote; a 1967 film of that book, and then two more movies — "Capote" in 2005 and "Infamous" the next year — which examined the killings and Capote's actions reporting on them.

Yet for all the detail widely available now, there is more. The transcript of a habeas corpus proceeding on behalf of Hickock and Smith fills more than 1,400 pages. It's filled with details about the crime and the subsequent investigation.

A habeas corpus proceeding is common in cases in which prisoners take issue with some aspect of their incarceration. Because several of the correctional facilities in the Leavenworth area lie within the jurisdiction of the U.S. District Court for the District of Kansas, Topeka Division, the Central Plains Region has transcripts and documents from many such proceedings.

The Hickock and Smith hearings took place on different occasions from July to November 1963. They covered details of Hickock's and Smith's arrest in Las Vegas, Nevada, and their interrogation by members of the Kansas Bureau of Investigation. In one session, Smith and his attorney appeared to be alleging that KBI agents used wrong procedures in questioning of Smith.

At one point, Smith's lawyer led his client through the car trip with KBI agents from Las Vegas back to Garden City, Kansas.

Q. And that the trip took approximately two days, is that right?

A. Yes, sir.

Q. I believe you also stated that there were two other people in the car with you.

A. There was.

Q. Both of them — both of whom — were K.B. I. agents, is that right?

A. That's right, sir.

Q. And that they were constantly talking to you, questioning you during the time that you were en route in the automobile.

A. That is right, sir.

Q. I believe that you stated that a part of the time you and your car were following the car with Mr. Hickock in it.

A. Yes, sir, that is right.

Q. And that these officers would point up there and tell you that, when they saw Hickock talking to another officer, that he had already confessed and had told them that you had murdered all four of the Clutter family, is that correct?

A. That's right, sir.

These proceeding didn't alter the end of the story. In April 1965 Hickock and Smith died by hanging at the Kansas state prison in Lansing.

And they refused it--to acknowledge any request on
counsel.

Q.   All right. Well, did they tell you that all the
had was just a few questions?

A.   They said they had a few questions to ask me.
They wouldn't answer in regard to my request for
counsel, that I wanted counsel before I made any
statements at all. And they just interrogated u
questioned me.

Q.   All right. At any time while you were in jail
at Las Vegas, whether it is three days or four d
or however long it was, did you--were you ever
granted your request for an attorney?

A.   No, sir; it was never mentioned again that they
would ever--they never said that I could have co
They never gave me an opportunity to have counsel.
And I requested it two or three times, that I wanted
counsel before I was questioned or anything, made
any statements.

Q.   Now, is that the way you started out these interrogations
that they gave you?

A.   Yes, sir.

Q.   That before you talked to them you wanted an attorney.

A.   Yes, sir.

Q.   And, how many times, if you recall, during the first

Perry Smith testified about his request
for a lawyer.
Record Group 21

THE BIG PICTURE

Downtown movie theaters were bad for business.

At least, that was the conventional wisdom in 1913 when the Royal Theater opened in the 1000 block of Main Street in Kansas City.

Nearby business owners thought films would wind up clearing the sidewalk of shoppers for two hours at a time. At one point, Kansas City ordinances prohibited movie houses downtown.

When entrepreneur Frank L. Newman first applied for a permit to build the Royal Theater, it was denied. Eventually he won, but then found himself in a new dispute

The Royal Theater often mounted on its canopy huge displays booming movies and their stars. The owner of an adjacent building housing a shoe store took the theater operators to federal court, arguing that the outsized displays limited visibility of the shoe store.

The plaintiff hired a photographer who documented the displays over several months in 1926. The pictures showed huge and distracting signs representing Harold Lloyd and Douglas Fairbanks, Clara Bow and Greta Nissen.

In 1931 a federal judge ruled that while the plaintiff had an "easement of light" that couldn't lawfully be impaired by the adjoining theater's canopy, he wasn't entitled to relief, given that the canopy only "immaterially" intercepted that light.

Arguably, retail interests prevailed in the end. The theater closed and the building was remodeled for store space in the 1930s.

Today, the photographs generated by the litigation open a window into time, showing everyday life on Main Street. They show not only that film studios budgeted large sums for advertising but also that most men wore hats and that automobiles had become common enough that parking had to be regulated.

This and following pages: Massive ad campaigns staged by this Main Street movie house. The complainant's photographer also documented the entire west side on the 1000 block of Main Street.
Record Group 21

A BUMP ON THE ROAD TO FAME

In 1962, federal authorities charged a young Omaha man with preparing fake draft cards. The indictment was a low moment in the life of Nick Nolte, former college football player, but he survived that brush with the law and went on to fame as an actor on television and in the movies.

Nolte, who had just turned 21, faced five counts of "aiding and abetting the making of false identification and representation." According to the indictment, he had supplied federal documents that could be used as draft cards to five individuals in Omaha and Lincoln, Nebraska, in summer and fall 1960.

Papers generated by *United States of America v. Nicholas King Nolte* include a 1962 arrest warrant, the indictment, and a receipt for it, signed by Nolte and his lawyer.

Nolte grew up in Omaha and played football in high school and at Arizona State University. He was uninterested in attending classes, and drifted from college to college before the indictment. About the same time, a friend took him to see a production of "Death of a Salesman" in California. That experience is said to have filled Nolte with resolve to pursue acting as a career.

First, however, the federal charges had to be dealt with. He received three years probation on each on three counts, to run concurrently.

In 1976 Nolte became familiar to television audiences through his role in "Rich Man, Poor Man."

IN THE UNITED STATES DISTRICT COURT FOR THE

DISTRICT OF NEBRASKA

UNITED STATES OF AMERICA,   )
)
            Plaintiff,   )   CR. 0753
)
        vs.   )
)
NICHOLAS KING NOLTE,   )   JUDGMENT AND
)
            Defendant.   )   ORDER OF PROBATION
_____)

On March 7, 1963, came the attorney for the United

States, Frederic J. Coufal, Assistant United States Attorney

for the District of Nebraska, and the defendant NICHOLAS KING

NOLTE appeared in person and with his attorney, Richard M.

Fellman, a member of the Bar of this Court.

The defendant NICHOLAS KING NOLTE entered a plea of

guilty to the Counts I, II, and III contained in the Indictment,

to wit:

> COUNT I: That during the month of June, 1960, at Omaha,
> Douglas County, Nebraska, within the District of Nebraska,
> NICHOLAS KING NOLTE did knowingly transfer and deliver to
> another, to wit, Gary Francis Byrne, for the purpose of
> aiding and abetting the making of false identification
> and representation, a blank Selective Service Registration
> Certificate, which the said defendant then knew would be
> used in making false identification and representation.
> In violation of Title 50 App. United States Code,
> Section 462.

> COUNT II: That during the month of October, 1960, at Omaha,
> Douglas County, Nebraska, within the District of Nebraska,
> NICHOLAS KING NOLTE did knowingly transfer and deliver to
> another, to wit, Judd Frederick Wagner, for the purpose of
> aiding and abetting the making of false identification and
> representation, a blank Selective Service Registration
> Certificate, which the said defendant then knew would be
> used in making false identification and representation.

> In violation of Title 50 App. United States Code,
> Section 462.

> COUNT III: That on or about October 28, 1960, at Lincoln,
> Lancaster County, Nebraska, within the District of Nebraska,
> NICHOLAS KING NOLTE did knowingly transfer and deliver to
> another, to wit, Gregg Allen Andreasen, for the purpose of
> aiding and abetting the making of false identification and
> representation, a blank Selective Service Registration

Papers from future star Nick Nolte's early run-in with the law.
Record Group 21

PROTECTING A DETECTIVE'S GOOD NAME

Long before Americans associated pulp fiction with film director Quentin Tarantino, there was Nick Carter.

By the early 1900s the fictional young detective was familiar to readers across the country. They followed his adventures in publications distributed by Street & Smith, a New York publishing firm.

In 1912 Street & Smith filed a complaint in St. Louis federal court against the Atlas Manufacturing Co. for selling detective stories with the familiar "Nick Carter" name. Street & Smith had registered that name as a trademark with the U.S. Patent Office in 1910. Street & Smith estimated the value of the good will and reputation enjoyed by the "Nick Carter" detective stories at $1 million.

Over time they may have been worth more than that. One scholar considers Nick Carter, whose first adventure appeared in 1886, the most published character in American literature. By the 1940s the character had his own radio series, "Nick Carter, Master Detective," and also appeared in films. Later, Nick evolved into a spy whose adventures were distributed in paperback novels.

In 1912 the court sided with Street & Smith, and granted an injunction against Atlas Manufacturing.

Street & Smith's pride and joy, Nick Carter
Record Group 21

No. 14   DEC. 14, 1912   5 CENTS

NICK CARTER
STORIES
REG. U. S. PAT. OFF.

THE SILENT PASSENGER

STREET & SMITH
PUBLISHERS
NEW YORK

WHEN NICK CARTER GAVE
HIS NAME, THE WOMAN, PEERING
THROUGH HER VEIL, CAUGHT HER
BREATH AT THE SOUND OF IT.

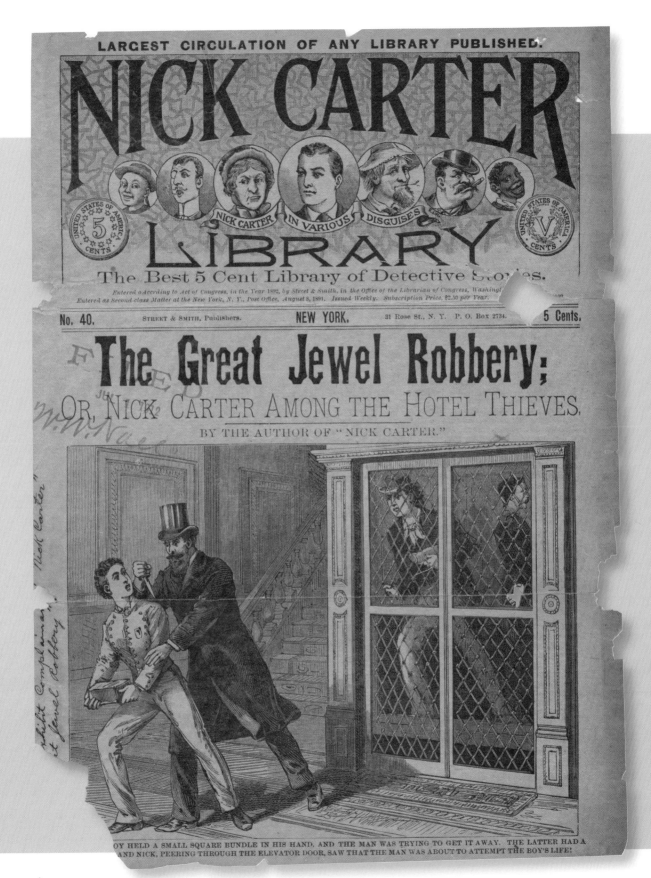

LARGEST CIRCULATION OF ANY LIBRARY PUBLISHED.

NICK CARTER

NICK CARTER IN VARIOUS DISGUISES

UNITED STATES OF AMERICA 5 CENTS

UNITED STATES OF AMERICA V CENTS

LIBRARY

The Best 5 Cent Library of Detective Stories.

Entered according to Act of Congress, in the Year 1892, by Street & Smith, in the Office of the Librarian of Congress, Washington.
Entered as Second-class Matter at the New York, N. Y., Post Office, August 8, 1891. Issued Weekly. Subscription Price, $2.50 per Year.

| No. 40. | STREET & SMITH, Publishers. | NEW YORK. | 31 Rose St., N. Y. P. O. Box 2734. | 5 Cents. |

The Great Jewel Robbery;
OR, NICK CARTER AMONG THE HOTEL THIEVES.

BY THE AUTHOR OF "NICK CARTER."

...OY HELD A SMALL SQUARE BUNDLE IN HIS HAND, AND THE MAN WAS TRYING TO GET IT AWAY. THE LATTER HAD A
...AND NICK, PEERING THROUGH THE ELEVATOR DOOR, SAW THAT THE MAN WAS ABOUT TO ATTEMPT THE BOY'S LIFE!

A TREE WITH OUR NAME....

In 1916 Stark Bros. Nurseries & Orchards Co., a northeastern Missouri company known for its tree and fruit catalogs, sued William P. Stark Nurseries — in the opposite corner of the state — for infringing on its registered "Stark Trees" trademark.

Yes, the court found, there had been infringement. But should damages should be limited to the date when Stark Bros. notified the other Stark that its trademark was registered? That question made it to the U.S. Supreme Court, which in 1921 determined that it was a trademark registrant's duty to notify the public of the trademark.

Among exhibits for the trial were Stark Bros. catalogs of the era. Today, these catalogs — with their beautiful, appetizing illustrations of fruits — are pursued by collectors.

Stark Bros. Nurseries & Orchards Co. still operates in Louisiana, Missouri, and customers can get catalogs by visiting the company website.

Copyright, 1910, by Stark Bro's Nurseries and Orchards Co.

Stark Delicious
(One-half natural size)

| Washington Grown | New York Grown | Iowa Grown, from the |
| New Mexico Grown | Colorado Grown | original tree |

IN THE DISTRICT COURT OF THE UNITED STATES FOR THE SOUTHWESTERN

DIVISION OF THE WESTERN DISTRICT OF MISSOURI

```
--------------------------------
Stark Bros. Nurseries &          0
Orchards Company,                0
                Complainant,     0
                                 0        In Equity
     -vs-                         0
                                 0        No. 18
William P. Stark and William     0
H. Stark, Trustees, doing        0
business under the name and      0
style of William P. Stark        0
Nurseries,                       0
                Defendant.       0
--------------------------------
```

D E C R E E

     This cause having come on to be heard upon

the pleadings and proofs, and counsel for the respective parties

having been heard, and the court being fully advised in the

premises, now, upon consideration thereof,

              IT IS ORDERED, ADJUDGED AND DECREED

that the name "Stark Trees" has been a trade-mark upon fruit

trees and nursery products for twenty-five years last past;

that on June 24, 1913, said trade-mark was duly registered under

the ten year clause of the Act of Congress of February 20, 1905,

in the United States Patent Office, and is a valid and subsisting

1 June Elberta
2 Elberta Cling
3 October Elberta
4 Elberta
5 Stark Early Elberta

Copyright, 1910, by Stark Bro's Nurseries and Orchards Co.

Three-fourths natural size

68

STUNG

It's no wonder that sports leagues keep gamblers at arm's length. A century ago, the fix was frequently on, and unwitting bettors were the victims. In western Iowa in 1909, a court heard complaints that organizers of prize fights and wrestling matches were controlling the results to bilk bettors.

In fact, the years just before and after World War I were the golden age of sports betting schemes. One reason: communication was slower. According to *The Big Con,* a 1940 history of confidence men, fixers could operate in the crucial interval between the actual end of, say, a horse race and the arrival of the result by telegraph. David Maurer, a University of Louisville linguist, wrote *The Big Con,* which details schemes that closely resemble the fix described in the 1973 movie, "The Sting." Maurer wrote the book because he was fascinated by the jargon of the confidence men. The deception involving horse races and the telegraph was known as the "wire." That was the first of the big con games, perfected just before 1900.

Such gangs often operated "stores," where schemes played out like theatrical productions in buildings that looked like mercantile stores. The "store" might contain actual merchandise but its real business was swindling unwitting victims, "marks."

Those Iowa prize fights and wrestling matches were detailed in *United States v. John C. Mabray, et al,* conceding that Mabray, one of many defendants, might not be the defendant's real name. Con men, it was alleged, convinced victims that they were privy to inside information, which flattered them. Later, after the swindle was done, the marks often were embarrassed to come forward and admit their naivete.

One such mark, however, did come forward. Court documents say that Samuel Sutor of Cass County, Minnesota, had come to Council Bluffs, Iowa, and not long afterward written a friend at home asking that $5,000 be withdrawn from his bank account.

"I have a legitimate deal on hand whereby I can make a good sum of money," Sutor wrote.

Eventually, several of the defendants were found guilty and sentenced.

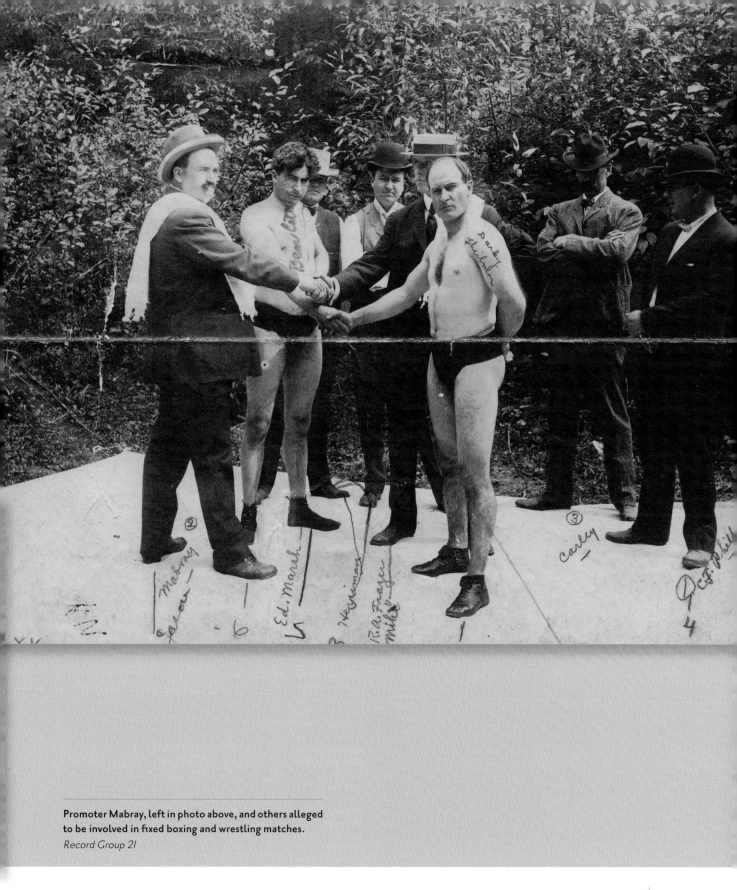

Promoter Mabray, left in photo above, and others alleged
to be involved in fixed boxing and wrestling matches.
Record Group 21

CURLEE
CLOTHING COMPANY

FACTORY NO. 4.

A B

C

CHILDREN'S CHRISTMAS PARTY
DONNELLY GARMENT CO.
PLA-MOR   DEC. 19, 1936

Ex. 25
M.B.M.

IN AND OUT OF FASHION

Kansas City and St. Louis once boasted large
fashion and apparel industries.

After the Civil War, St. Louis represented the largest inland
cotton market in the world. As for Kansas City, it benefited
from a decision by U.S. immigration in the early 1900s to open
a point of entry in Galveston, Texas. Through that door came
a stream of European immigrants, many of whom found their
way to Kansas City. Tailoring and dressmaking had taken hold
before the turn of the century and by 1955 about 150 Kansas
City garment firms employed more than 8,000 workers.
The Central Plains Region files contain graphic evidence
of battles waged in the fashion industry, from union
representation to disputes over hair curler design — and
even to the bankruptcy of a Kansas City clothing merchant
who would one day influence world politics.

GETTING VIOLENT

In 1925 members of the Amalgamated Clothing Workers of America called for a strike against the Curlee Clothing Company of St. Louis.

That June, union members picketed outside the company's doors. According to the company's president, however, they did more than that. Company employees, he said, were "repeatedly assaulted and outraged and insulted" while trying to go to and from work.

An assault on one company employee was captured by a photographer as it occurred. Other Curlee employees who said they had been attacked posed for photographers to show their injuries.

The company sought a restraining order and injunction against the union, which a court issued in November 1925. Two years later a federal appeals court affirmed the decision.

St. Louis clothing workers marched outside Curlee's plant, above. Sometimes, strikers and non-strikers came to blows, left.

Record Group 21

STATE OF MISSOURI, |
                   | ss.
CITY OF ST.LOUIS. |

  Before me, Jennie R.Frame, a Notray Public, within and for the City of St.Louis,Missouri, personally appeared, VENZIE FERRERI, who being first duly sworn on her oath did state:

  My name is Venzie Ferreri and I live at 1018 North Tenth Street, and am employed on the fifth floor of the Curlee Clothing Company factry at 21st and Locust Street, for over a year:

  I recognize and idenify the accompanying photographs A and B as being true pictures taken of myself at my home on Wednesday morning July 15,1925, two days after I had been assaulted on Tenth Street between Wash and Franklin by three girl strikers whose name I later found out to be Lena Bono, May Nichols and Lee Daniels. At the time of the assault, whih occurred on Monday Monring July 13,1925, at 7.30 A.M. I was on my way to work accompanied by Anna Shirano, of 1008 North Tenth Street who was employed on the third floor of the Curlee Clothing Company factory at 21st and Locust Street where she has worked for about three years. Exhibit A, is a true picture showing the discoloration of my left eye, commonly known as a black eye, which was caused by being struck with the fist of one of the three girls who assaulted Anna Shirano and myself on that date. Exhibit B is a true picture showing the swelling on my right foot caused by one of these three girl strikers who stamped on my foot which gave me such great pain that I was obliged to stay away from work for two weeks. All three of the girls who assaulted us were arrested. During the assault a twenty dollar pair of glasses were knocked from my eyes and I have never recovered them.

         Venzi Ferreri

  Subscribed and sworn to before me this 7th day of July,1925.

  My term expires December19,1925.

         Jennie R.Frame,
         Notary Public.

STATE OF MISSOURI)
) ss.
CITY OF ST. LOUIS)

On this 8th day of August, 1925, before me,
William P. Carleton, a Notary Public within and for the
City of St. Louis, State of Missouri, personally appeared
Vita and Mary Bono, who, being first by me duly sworn, upon
their oaths state:

Our names are Vita and Mary Bono. We live at 2409
Coleman Street and are employed on the fifth floor of the Curlee
Clothing Company factory at 21st and Locust Street, where we have
both worked for over a year.

We recognize and identify the accompanying photograph,
marked 2409 Coleman Street, as being a true picture taken of the
front window of our home which is in the first floor of the building at 2409 Coleman Street, taken on Monday morning, June 16th,
1925, the next day after all the glass in these windows, with the
exception of the fancy colored glass at the upper corners of the
window frame, had been broken by rocks thrown by unidentified
parties at 1 o'clock a. m. on June 14th, 1925, which was on Sunday.

Five strikers came to our house at 7:30 p. m. on
Thursday evening, June 4th, 1925, among them were Vito Larosa,
Sebastian Bono, Sam Loporto, and Vito Ferreri. Vito Larosa
and Sam Loporto did most of the talking. They wanted us to join
them and go out on strike, but we refused. Vito Larosa then
said "Curlee watches the factory in the day time, but no one watches
your home at night." The morning on which the glass in all
the windows in the front of our home was broken was exactly 10
days after the threat made by Larosa. It may be noted that there
are six panes of glass in all which were broken by the parties
who threw the rocks and also the screen which protects the central
window. We have never had any enemies and cannot understand why
our windows were broken unless by strikers.

Vita Bono

Mary Bono

Subscribed and sworn to before me this 8th day of
August, 1925.
My commission expires June 18, 1929.

William P. Carleton
Notary Public.

WPC

Accusations of intimidation and injury
flew through the Curlee clothing
dispute.
Record Group 21

UNION VS. MANAGEMENT

The Donnelly Garment Company once ranked as a powerhouse of the apparel industry in Kansas City. In 1937, it had about 1,300 employees.

That year the company filed suit in federal court seeking a restraining order against the International Ladies' Garment Workers Union. Union officers, Donnelly officials contended, were trying to infiltrate the company.

The dispute lasted about a decade and sometimes turned violent, as captured in photographs of the era.

The pictures contrast considerably with warm memories that many former employees have of working at Donnelly. A 2006 documentary film, "Nelly Don: A Stitch in Time," played for several months to Kansas City audiences whose members either had worked for the company or had relatives who worked there. The film included vintage footage of Donnelly apparel assembly, as well as of models wearing individual designs.

The film, produced by a great-grandnephew of Nell Donnelly Reed, the company founder, described Donnelly Garment as forward-thinking in its treatment of employees, offering benefits that convinced many they didn't need union representation.

In 1946, a federal appeals turned down Donnelly's request for an injunction against the union. Ultimately, in the 1960s, company employees chose ILGWU membership, but by then Nell Donnelly Reed — "Nelly Don" as Reed was known — had sold the company.

She died in 1991 at age 102.

The 2006 documentary also offered an unexpected footnote about David Q. Reed, Reed's son, a Kansas City lawyer who died in 1999. Many believed David had been adopted by the garment manufacturer during a trip to Europe in 1931. In fact, she had delivered the infant in a Chicago hospital.

The father was former U.S. senator from Missouri, James A. Reed. Both had been married to others at the time. They married in 1933, after Reed's first wife died and Nelly Don divorced her first husband.

Scuffles with police erupted outside Donnelly Garment in 1937, only months after the company-sponsored children's Christmas party, top.
Record Group 21

CHILDREN'S CHRISTMAS PARTY
DONNELLY GARMENT Co.
PLA-MOR   DEC 19, 1936

THE PRESIDENT'S OLD PARTNER

What Harry Truman didn't go through, Eddie Jacobson did.

The two World War I Army buddies were partners in Truman & Jacobson, a downtown Kansas City haberdashery. The store, which opened in 1919, did well at first. But a nationwide recession hurt the Kansas City retail apparel business and the two closed the shop in September 1922.

Filing for bankruptcy in 1925, Jacobson declared debts of $10,676.50 compared to $507 in assets. That included $280 in household goods — which consisted of a sewing machine, dishes and kitchen utensils — and $28 in cash. Jacobson's Army uniform, he claimed, was exempt under Missouri law.

Truman, meanwhile, tried politics. In 1922, the same year the haberdashery closed, voters elected him Eastern Jackson County Judge, an administrative position. He did not declare bankruptcy. Through the years — as Truman was elected Jackson County presiding judge and then U.S. senator — Truman and Jacobson remained poker buddies.

After Truman became president in 1945 Jacobson, who was Jewish, began receiving requests to influence his friend about the future of Palestine. Ultimately Jacobson traveled to Washington to ask Truman to receive Zionist leader Chaim Weizmann. Truman did, and assured Weizmann that he would work toward the establishment and recognition of a Jewish state. Truman issued de facto recognition of Israel in 1948.

Jacobson died in 1955. Today an auditorium bearing his name stands in a Tel Aviv B'nai B'rith building.

Harry Truman's former business partner, Eddie Jacobson, seeking a discharge of debts.
Record Group 21

IN THE DISTRICT COURT OF THE UNITED STATES

FOR THE WESTERN DISTRICT OF MISSOURI.

In the Matter of   .

EDWARD JACOBSON,   .   In Bankruptcy

                                    .
          Bankrupt   .

To the Honorable A. L. Reeves,

          Judge of the District Court of the United States

               for the Western District of Missouri.

          Edward Jacobson, of Kansas City, in the county of
Jackson, and State of Missouri, in said district, respectfully represents that on the 10th day of February, last
past, he was duly adjudged bankrupt under the acts of Congress
relating to bankruptcy; that he has duly surrendered all his
property and rights of property, and has fully complied with
all the requirements of said acts and the orders of the court
touching his bankruptcy.

          Wherefore he prays that he may be decreed by the court
to have a full discharge from all debts probable against his
estate under such bankruptcy acts, except such debts as are
excepted by law from such discharge.

Dated this 3/st day of March, 1925.

                              Edward Jacobson
                                   Bankrupt

WHOSE WAVE IS IT?

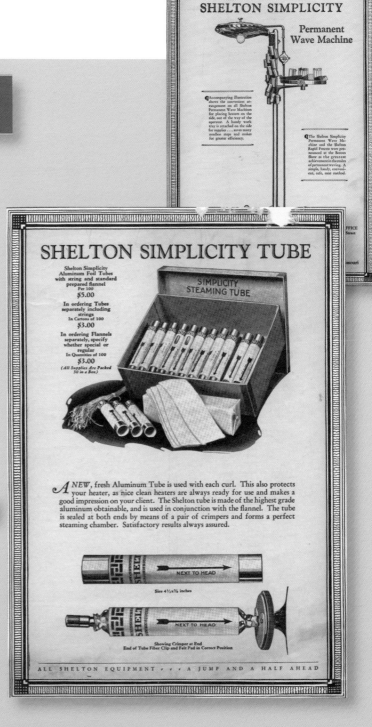

The flapper era of the 1920s was a good time to hold a patent on a device that could create so-called permanent waves in women's hair.

The S. Lemur Company was happy to have such a patent, and unhappy enough with the W.G. Shelton Company's own permanent wave instrument to sue. In 1927, the two companies squared off in federal court, Lemur claiming that Shelton's waving tubes were too similar to theirs. Customers, Lemur said, were "being deceived to believe that the tubes of the plaintiff's manufacture are being used on their hair."

The court disagreed. End of complaint.

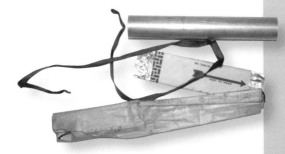

The permanent wave tube and the company's supporting materials for hairdressers.

Record Group 21

THE SHELTON GIRL

*T*HIS *Oil Painting*, 16½x22½ inches, in full color, supplied free with each
Shelton Simplicity Permanent Wave Machine. Makes beautiful display
under electric light for show window purposes. Picture, to obtain the best
effect, should be framed. Extra copies may be secured at $10.00 each.

ALL SHELTON EQUIPMENT ↯ ↯ ↯ A JUMP AND A HALF AHEAD

Stuck in sand on road in Cimarron county, Okla. Many dust bowl roads are made impassable by drifting sand.

Submitted by:

Ivy M. Howard
Box 323
Stillwater, Oklahoma

8.

MISCELLANY

Deep in the Dust Bowl, 1936.
Record Group 114

MARAUDERS FROM THE NORTH?

Under the category of being prepared for just about everything, file this item.

In 1919 officers with the U.S. Army Corps of Engineers made plans to defend North Dakota and Montana against an invasion from Canada. In a 1976 article in *North Dakota History*, historian Lawrence Larsen, using papers that came to the Central Plains Region branch in 1970, described the contingency plans in detail. They included artillery pieces mounted on railroad cars that could be moved depending on their target.

What Larsen couldn't find was any compelling reason for the planners to fear an invasion from the north.

"Were thousands of Mounties preparing to gallop south toward Bismarck?" Larsen asked. "Did Bolshevik hordes propose to attack via the North Pole?"

Perhaps, Larsen wrote, those involved were simply doing their patriotic duty. It was also possible, he added, that with World War I having recently ended and the U.S. Army facing possible cuts in the officers corps, the planning "may have been a case of work for work's sake."

Railcar-mounted artillery.
Record Group 77

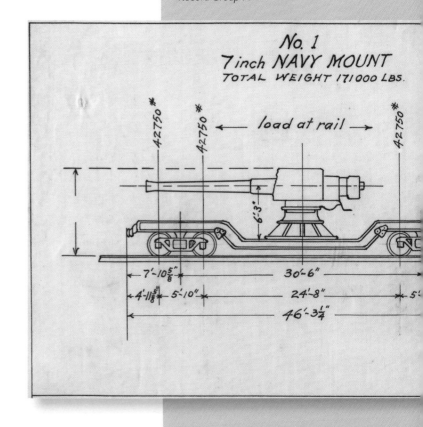

DATA SHEETS

for

RAILWAY ARTILLERY ARMAMENT

*   *   *

GUN NO.I

7" Gun, Navy, on 7" Army Railway Carriage, Model 1918 MI.

Maximum Range:- 17,000 Yds.

Length and size of ties necessary for firing positions:- Standard.

Weight of rails necessary for firing positions:- 60 lbs. to yard.

Special ballasting required for firm positions:- None.

Type of emplacement:- Car is raised by four built in screw jacks. Steel
                     "H" beams and wood cross ties are placed. Car is
                     then lowered and outriggers set.

GUN. NO.2.

8" Gun Model 1888 on 8" Backette Carriage, Model 1918.

Maximum range:- 23,940 Yds.

Ties required for firing position:- Standard.

Weight of rail required for firing position:- 60 lbs. per yard.

Special ballasting required for firing position:- None.

Type of emplacement:- Car is raised by four built in screw jacks. Steel
                      "H" beams and wood cross ties are then placed un-
                      der car. Car is then lowered and outriggers set.

Size of level ground needed for emplacement:- 40' wide, 60' long.

GUN NO.3.

12" Mortar, Model 1890 MI, on 12" Mortar Railway Carriage, Model 1918.

Maximum range:- 15,291 Yards.

Size of ties for firing position:- Standard.

Weight of rail for firing position:- 60 lbs.per yard.

Special ballasting for firing position:- None.

Size of level ground needed for emplacement:- 40' wide, 60' long.

Type of emplacement:- Car is raised by four built in screw jacks. A plat-
                      form of longitudinal "H" beams and wooden cross ties
                      is placed. The car is lowered onto this platform
                      and the outriggers set.

GUN NO.4.

16" Howitzer, Model E on 16" Howitzer Railway Carriage, Model 1918 MI

Maximum range:-   45° - 23,230 yds.
                   25° - 13,900 yds

Minimum radius of Epi required:- 100 yds.

TAKING IT TO THE STREETS

By the beginning of the 20th century, city health officials largely accepted the bacterial theory of disease and identified the fly as a major carrier, according to researchers Joel Tarr and Clay McShane. Flies buzzed around piles of manure, which were common sights in streets of the Gilded Age, when horses or mules pulled most loads.

Enter street flushing, the technology of which was in dispute in *American Street Flushing Company v. St. Louis Street Flushing Machine Company*, a lawsuit heard in St. Louis federal court in 1906. The question: Had patents held by American Street Flushing been infringed upon by St. Louis Street Flushing?

After trial proceedings whose records fill several boxes, the court ruled in favor of the complainant, American Street Flushing.

Among exhibits in the case were several photos showing street flushers in action and sometimes their means of propulsion — ironically, horses or mules.

Spraying the streets of St. Louis.
Record Group 21

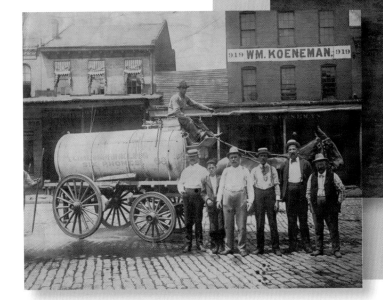

FOR THE SAKE OF CONVENIENCE...

Verne Sankey worked hard at his ransom notes.

The former South Dakota rancher was arrested in Chicago in January 1934, and he confessed to the kidnapping of two wealthy men: Charles Boettcher of Denver and Haskell Bohn of St. Paul.

Among the evidence gathered by the government were several ransom notes sent to the Boettcher family along with drafts of other notes that someone — probably Sankey — had found wanting and revised, striking out entire paragraphs.

Then there is another ransom note in which blanks appear, apparently in the interest of efficiency, allowing the letter to be customized with the name of the victim. "Do not notify police," it read, "if you do, and they start making it hot for us, you will never see _____ alive again. We are holding _____ for Sixty Thousand Dollars."

Sankey received $60,000 for the release of Boettcher.

After apprehending Sankey in Chicago, federal officers searching his apartment found another kidnapping letter again threatening the Boettcher family. Sankey, however, said he wrote the letter "to while away idle hours" while hiding from police and he denied planning a second kidnapping of the Denver man.

A few days after his arrest, Sankey hanged himself in his jail cell in Sioux City, South Dakota.

Rough draft and completed fill-in-the-blank ransom note.
Record Group 21

r 100,000.00 dollars ransom.

this money in ten and twenty dollar

be old bills only.

noney ready and are willing to ~~pay~~

d if you ~~gives~~ for the safe return

then ~~p~~ insert the fo

s. (Please write

~~sign~~ ~~I l you~~

stand that we are not

captured while clo

your mind ~~slight~~

pay the above or

off at once as we

present condition

letters with the mon

sending this letter

ect to see ——— you

he wouldn't stand

oo are smart enoug

e be if you try that

these two courses. E

ransom, Or forget it all.

L. J. Hedley. 3/5-33

C. V. Satt. 3/5/33

To whom it may concern.

Do not notify police, If you do,and theystart making it hot
for us, you will never see_____alive again.
We are holding_____for Sixty Thousand Dollars.
We are asking you to get this money in Ten and Twenty dollar
bills and they must be old bills only.
 When you get this money ready and are willing to pay as above
for the safe return of _____,then insert the following add
in the Denver Post, personal items.

(Please write, I am ready to return)
sign (Mabel)

Now we want you to understand that we are not going to take
any chance of being captured while closing this deal, so you
can make up your mind here and now that you will either pay
the above, or that _____ will never be returned.
Keep all of my letters as they must all be returned to me with
the money.
We will not stand for any stalling thru advise that police
may give you.
You are smart enough to know what the results will be if you
try that.
You know what happened to little Charles Lindberg through his
 father calling the police' He would be alive today if his
father had followed instructions given him.
You are to choose one of these to courses,Either insert add
and be prepared to pay ransome, Or forget it all.

P off 24 /800

Filed Oct 23 1934.
Roy B. Marker,
Clerk.
By C. C. Schwarz,
Deputy

Filed May 11. 1934
Roy B Marker
Clerk.

MY LETTERHEAD, MY COMPANY

At some point, staff members at the Central Plains Region decided that many of the archived letters in their care were interesting for the way they looked, beyond whatever message they conveyed. Letterheads often bore fascinating detail or whimsical design. So the staff made a collection of them.

Today these documents can be considered the corporate websites of their time, presenting the public faces of private companies and government agencies.

One thing stands out: Companies often were proud of their buildings and so reproduced likenesses of them on their stationery.

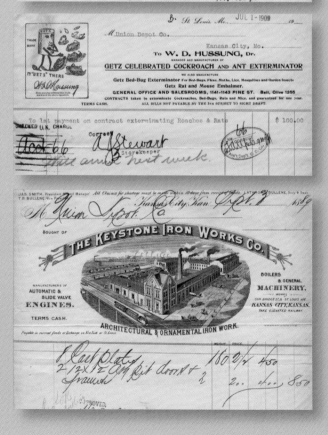

With their letterheads companies strutted their institutional pride.
Record Group 21

FIFTH AVENUE HOTEL

Terms Three Dollars per Day.

Corner Fifth Avenue and Quincy Street.

J. B. FLUNO, Proprietor.

Topeka, Kansas, Jan'y 19th 1874

A. S. Thomas

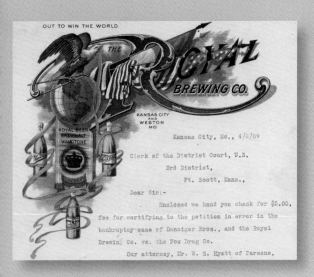

OUT TO WIN THE WORLD

THE ROYAL BREWING CO.

KANSAS CITY AND WESTON MO.

ROYAL BEER
BREWMALT
VIVA-TONE

Kansas City, Mo., 4/2/09

Clerk of the District Court, U.S.
3rd District,
Ft. Scott, Kans.,

Dear Sir:-

Enclosed we hand you check for $5.00,
fee for certifying to the petition in error in the
bankruptcy case of Danciger Bros., and the Royal
Brewing Co. vs. the Fox Drug Co.

Our attorney, Mr. W. S. Hyatt of Parsons,

Scott Paper Co.

MAKERS OF TOILET PAPER

SEVENTH and GLENWOOD AVENUE

PHILADELPHIA

BALSAM
SANITISSUE
FRAGRANT·HEALING
Scott Paper Co.
PHILADELPHIA, PA.

SOLD TO

NEW YORK OFFICE,
12 Vesey Street,

CHICAGO OFFICE,
160 STATE STREET.

TERMS, 30 DAYS.

ST. LOUIS OFFICE, 420 N. THIRD STREET

RECEIVED
MAY 16 1910

Office of W. W. COOK,

REAL ESTATE AGENT

LIVE STOCK BROKER.

Medicine Lodge, Kansas, Feb'y ___ 188

THE GILLETTE-HERZOG MANUFACTURING Co.

STRUCTURAL AND ARCHITECTURAL ENGINEERS AND BRIDGE BUILDERS

Minneapolis, Minn., May 15/00 189

UNDER THE EAGLE'S WING

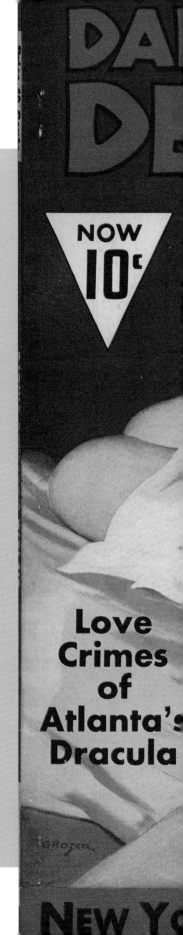

Did creators of the New Deal support *Hooey* magazine?

Probably not. Nevertheless, the editors of the mildly risqué cartoon magazine displayed on its cover the eagle emblem of the National Recovery Administration. By doing so, they suggested that the magazine's publisher met workplace standards mandated by the NRA, administrative arm of the National Industrial Recovery Act.

That act was one of several New Deal measures approved after Roosevelt's election in 1932 to stimulate recovery from the Great Depression. The act authorized codes to reduce unemployment and fight unfair business practices, and also set wage and hour standards.

Company executives who believed they met the regulations could display the NRA eagle emblem.

In 1935, however, NRA compliance officers investigated *Hooey's* publisher, Hart Publications of Long Prairie, Minnesota, apparently prompted by letters from Hart employees complaining of long hours and poor pay.

Today those letters are filed at the Central Plains Region branch, as are others defending the company as a locally owned business employing hundreds of Long Prairie area residents. Further, the correspondents argued, NRA regulations punished small towns like Long Prairie, which had a limited number of skilled workers. Hart Publications — which published not only magazines like *Hooey* and *Daring Detective Tabloid*, but also *Hardware World* and *Popular Aviation* — often had to pay overtime to meet deadlines. Publishing companies in bigger cities, these correspondents insisted, had a bigger pool of potential workers and didn't have to pay overtime.

The U.S. Supreme Court invalidated the National Recovery Act in 1935.

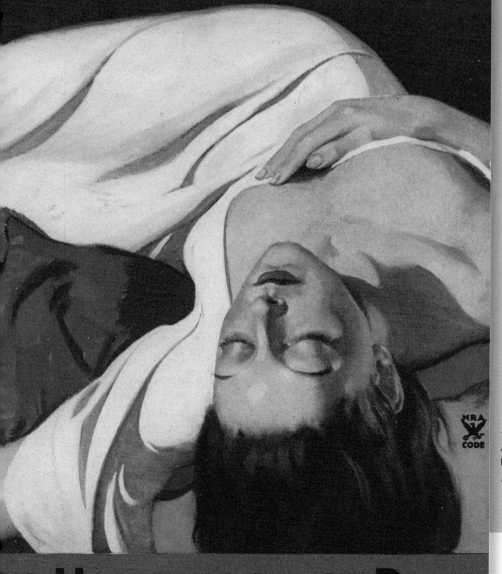

A Hart Publication product labeled at lower right with the NRA eagle.
Record Group 9

"Morning Gazette---

Lonely Hearts Talking"

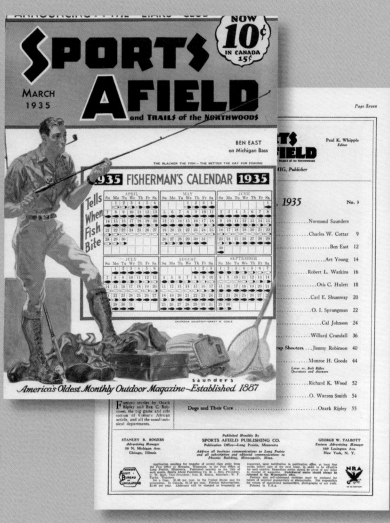

More covers, some colorful and some prosaic, from Hart Publications.

Record Group 9

MAKING MITTS BETTER

The nice pocket in your catcher's mitt didn't just happen.

It was put there by inventor Elroy Rogers in 1895. So went the claim of the Victor Sporting Goods Company of Massachusetts in a 1909 complaint against the Rawlings Manufacturing Company of St. Louis.

Victor submitted patent forms and drawings which, it believed, documented how improvements in catcher's mitts were the work of Rogers. According to documents filed with the U.S. Patent Office and submitted to federal court officials in St. Louis, Rogers' mitt was a novel and artful arrangement of rivets, buckles and loose straps. When secured and tightened in a specific way, the mitt could produce a proper pocket that could cradle a thrown baseball.

The patent documents assumed an audience knowledgeable in the sport.

"As is well known," read one document, "catcher's mitts as they come from the store are flat in the palm or side where the ball strikes and, being of a considerable thickness, the mitts cannot be doubled up by the hand to form a pocket. This is a serious defect in mitts, which players endeavor to remedy as soon as possible by repeated blows by the fist upon the mitt or by bending or punching it."

The Rogers improvements changed all that, the Victor company claimed, adding that Rawlings evidently was borrowing Rogers' work.

However, Victor's argument apparently was way too inside baseball. Ultimately the case was dismissed.

The Rogers mitt, with pocket and without.
Record Group 21

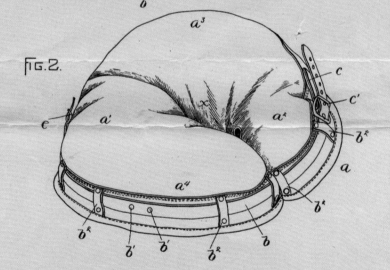

(No Model.)

E. L. ROGERS.
CATCHER'S GLOVE.

No. 540,514.   Patented June 4, 1895

Fig.1.

Fig.2.

WITNESSES:
A. D. Harrison
Rollin Abell

INVENTOR
Elroy L. Rogers
by Wright, Brown & Quinby
Attys.

FILED
APR 28 1909
James R. Gray
CLERK

THE NORRIS PETER CO., WASHINGTON, D. C.

Exhibit A.

GONE STRAIGHT – FOR A WHILE

In 1927 the warden of the federal penitentiary at Leavenworth received an unusual request from a former inmate, Frank "Monk" Trummer of Omaha, Nebraska. Trummer, who had entered the prison in 1920 for stealing interstate freight, told the warden he was embarking on a personal campaign against crime.

He was going on a speaking tour and needed photographs of himself as he appeared in Leavenworth. The warden supplied three pictures.

Trummer used the photographs in a poster that advertised his appearances. "I Paid the Full Penalty," read the poster, which depicted Trummer staring out from behind bars. "The awe-inspiring and true story of a man who has repented and gone straight."

Not forever, evidently. The last item in Trummer's file is another letter asking for a photograph — this time from a Nebraska deputy fire marshal.

"We have a warrant for this man's arrest for burning a canning factory at Auburn, Nebraska, and it is very important we locate a picture," the deputy marshal wrote in 1937.

Once again, the Leavenworth staff supplied a photo.

On the road with tales of punishment and repentance.
Record Group 129

"I PAID THE FULL PENALTY"

Says Frank "Monk" Trummer.   He will tell his thrilling story picturing the life and surroundings in a penitentiary

It will open your eyes, and give you the thrill of a lifetime

Men, Women, Boys and Girls should hear and see this Marvelous Entertainment

The awe-inspiring and true story of a man who has repented and has gone straight.

Entertainment and Education for the whole family

Completely illustrated on the Screen. - See why Crime doesn't pay.

BIG SCREEN PROGRAM

LEATRICE JOY in "Nobody's Widow"

No 8. "The Crimson Flash"- Special Comedy "The Big Idea"

Fox News showing latest Ocean Hops

FREMONT

THEATRE-Mon.-Tues. Sept. 19-20

8.

ritories. That is the important factor, how far they are from school.

Q. (By Mr. Bledsoe) Now, Mr. Brown, where do you live with reference to Monroe School?

A. Well, stated that I live at 511 West First Street which is fifteen blocks, approximately, from Monroe School.

        MR. GOODELL: I didn't get that.

        JUDGE MELLOTT: Fifteen blocks from Monroe School.

        THE WITNESS: Twenty-one blocks, pardon me; approximately twenty-one blocks.

Q. (By Mr. Bledsoe) You are talking about now the way your daughter has to travel to go to Monroe School, is that correct?

A. That is true.

Q. Does your daughter ride the school bus?

A. Yes.

Q. All right. Now, Mr. Brown, what time does your daughter leave home in the morning to walk to First and Quincy, the bus pick-up point, to go to school; what time does she leave home?

A. She leaves at twenty minutes 'till eight o'clock.

Q. Twenty minutes of eight.

A. Every school morning.

Q. What time, or thereabouts, does she board the bus at